Pelican Books
Intelligence and Personality

Born in London in 1913 of a French mother and a German father, Alice Heim gained a scholarship in Moral Sciences from Kingsley School, Hampstead, to Newnham College, Cambridge. Her Ph.D. thesis was in the border-zones of educational, vocational, industrial and clinical psychology.

Apart from a year spent at Stanford University, California, on a Smith-Mundt fellowship, Dr Heim has worked continuously in the Psychological Laboratory, Cambridge, as a member of the external scientific staff of the Medical Research Council. Her research work on individual differences in human psychology keeps her in close touch with schools, colleges of education, industry and clinical psychiatry. For many years she has taught in the University, directed and examined Ph.D. students, and conducted W.E.A. evening courses. She is a Fellow of Clare Hall, Cambridge. She is also a Fellow of the British Psychological Society, an Associate of Newnham College, and a member of the Editorial Advisory Panel of *Occupational Psychology*.

Dr Heim has published one previous book, *The Appraisal of Intelligence*, and some forty papers in English, French and American journals. The National Foundation for Educational Research have published three of her intelligence tests and one of interests and temperament. She is currently developing three further tests: on vocabulary, spatial perception and verbal reasoning.

Her outside interests include music, theatre, tennis, travel and work for the Cambridge Samaritans. She has two adopted children, one daughter and one son.

Alice Heim

Intelligence and Personality

Their Assessment and Relationship

Penguin Books

Penguin Books Ltd, Harmondsworth,
Middlesex, England
Penguin Books Inc., 7110 Ambassador Road,
Baltimore, Maryland 21207, U.S.A.
Penguin Books Australia Ltd, Ringwood,
Victoria, Australia

First published 1970
Reprinted 1971, 1974
Copyright © Alice Heim, 1970

Made and printed in Great Britain by
C. Nicholls & Company Ltd
Set in Monotype Times

For Jessica and Quentin

Contents

14 The Mediocrity of Women 136

Mediocrity of women
Cognitive differences between the sexes
Differences in temperament between the sexes
Inequality of opportunity

15 The Existence of Psychological Phenomena 146

Existence of psychological phenomena in their own right
How relevant is animal behaviour to human experience?
Application of 'experimental' to subject-matter rather than
    method
Widening the horizon of experimental psychology

People, you see, are so very different.

FYODOR DOSTOYEVSKY

When the heart comes into play, it numbs and paralyses the brain ...

Many things escape the reason, and a person who should attempt to understand life by merely using his reason would be like a man trying to take hold of a flame with the tongs. Nothing remains but a bit of charred wood, which immediately stops flaming ...

Everything which is created by the intelligence alone is false ...

There is no psychological truth unless it be particular; but on the other hand there is no art unless it be general. The whole problem lies just in that – how to express the general by the particular – how to make the particular express the general.

ANDRÉ GIDE

Acknowledgements

I should like to thank the following people for their help in preparing this book: Dr P. W. K. Stone for reading the manuscript at an early stage and clarifying the English in many places; Professor and Mrs H. L. Elvin, Professor M. D. Vernon and Mr D. L. Nuttall for useful constructive criticism. Miss K. P. Watts and Mrs V. Simmonds have also given a great deal of assistance at all stages. I should like, too, to express thanks to Mr E. G. Chambers for his help in making the Indexes and Mrs L. Turner for her impeccable typing. I am very grateful to the Medical Research Council for their encouragement and financial support over the years.

ALICE HEIM

Psychological Laboratory,
Cambridge.

May 1970

Note to the Reader

As a reader, I am often confused by the notation and the positioning of Notes and References in text-books. I have tried to make these as clear as possible in this book but I should like, nonetheless, to explain the system used.

I have written explanatory Notes, pages 155–88, to indicate briefly what is meant by certain psychological terms with which the layman may be unfamiliar. These are designated in the text by a small, raised, capital letter. Thus the small capital D in line 15 of page 18, immediately after 'behaviourists', indicates that an explanation of the term 'behaviourists' is available. As the book contains twenty-nine such notes, the last three are indicated with double letters AA, BB and CC.

References, pages 189–200, are designated in the text by small, raised arabic numerals, as in line 11 of page 14. It may be seen that the References are numbered within each chapter. References in the Notes, however, are indicated by footnotes on the relevant page.

There are two Indexes, one dealing with subject-matter and the other with authors.

1 Language and Concepts in Psychology

In the beginning was the word – ST JOHN

Language and concepts in psychology – The Subject –
Orexis – Against dichotomies

The words used by psychologists are a constant source of anxiety
to them and of rage to their readers (including other psychologists). If they coin a new term, in the belief that they have a new
concept, and wish it to be decently clad, it is often hailed as an
ugly and unnecessary neologism. If, on the other hand, they use
an already existing word and try to prune it or extend it to fit the
particular technical meaning they have in mind, they are liable
to be accused – often with justice – of debasing the language or
subtly misleading the reader.

This is a real difficulty, which obtains in all the sciences, but it
is perhaps at its worst in psychology; for that part of psychology
which is not concerned with rats or machines constantly needs to
refer to human beings and their attributes. There is an imposing
number of relevant terms in the English language – many of them
very vivid – but they tend to possess a generality and fluidity
which often makes them unsuitable. If the psychologist wishes
to write both precisely and readably about people, he is really in
trouble.

There are two words which occur again and again in this book
for which it is felt an apologetic explanation is required. The first
is the word 'Subject' and the second is 'orectic'. The former is an
example of a well-known, frequently used word, generally
written with a small s and, despite its several meanings, usually
unambiguous since its sense can almost always be inferred from
its context. In this book, the word is written with a capital letter
to denote the person taking a psychological test. There does not
appear to be any wholly satisfactory term for these all-essential
beings. 'Subjects' has been used throughout, in preference to

'testees' and to 'candidates' – the former of these having irrelevant associations and the latter suggesting that an academic examination or an application for a post is involved. It is felt that the capital letter is necessary in order to distinguish the term from 'subject' which occasionally appears in one of its other senses, as for instance in 'subject of specialization'.

The second term, 'orectic', requires a longer explanation, first because it does not appear at all in some dictionaries, secondly because when it is given (as, e.g. in the Shorter Oxford English Dictionary) its meaning differs from that given in dictionaries of psychology (such as Warren's[1] and Drever's[2]) and thirdly because the concept denoted by the term is a fairly complicated one. Despite these difficulties, I feel that the word is just what is needed for this book – in fact, its psychological meaning is absolutely essential to the main thesis.

Warren defines the noun, orexis, as 'the affective and conative aspects of experience as distinguished from the cognitive', Drever's definition is almost identical, save that he adds 'impulse, appetite, desire, emotion'. No doubt he would agree that this list is incomplete. He probably added those four attributes to help the non-psychologist who may be unfamiliar with the terms 'cognitive', 'affective' and 'conative'.

These three terms must be accepted if the meaning of 'orexis' (and its adjective 'orectic') is to be understood. 'Cognition' covers the thinking and knowing aspect of experience (problem-solving, recognizing, concept-forming); 'affect'* includes the emotional and feeling aspect (e.g. anger, fear, pleasure); 'conation' applies to the striving, doing aspect of experience (e.g. running a race, keeping order in the class-room, trying to attend to two things at once). Probably all human experiences include the three aspects, but their relative importance varies with the circumstances. To take as example a situation which is frequently cited in this book – sitting an intelligence test: the Subject *is aware that* he is taking a test and he *thinks about* the problems (cognition); he is also eager or apprehensive, co-operative or antagonistic, enjoying it or disliking it (affect); he may be putting forth *little effort* or he

*A noun, with the stress on the first syllable.

may be *striving to do well* (conation). The examples offered show how inseparable the three aspects are in practice.

It may be recalled that 'orectic' means 'the affective and conative aspects of experience as distinct from the cognitive'. I hope that the concept is now fairly clear and that the reader may wish to add to Drever's four-fold list such qualities as motivation, prejudice, mood, attitude.

Our main thesis is the inseparability of the three aspects of experience – for this book is concerned, unquestionably, as much with experience as it is with behaviour. Indeed, two of the three terms (affect and conation) have almost dropped out of psychological text books, though they used to figure largely in the days before rodentkind inherited experimental psychology from mankind. This change is due mainly to the increasingly strong emphasis on 'behaviour' *as opposed to* 'experience'. Nowadays, emotion for instance is exemplified by a defecating rat rather than an introspecting person. As the experimental psychologist is quick to point out, the latter 'might be lying' or 'might be mistaken' and, in any case, the extent of his emotion can scarcely be measured with the same accuracy as can the amount of rat faeces.

However, these two concepts (of affect and conation) jointly constitute 'orexis' and the term 'orectic' is used generally in preference to the term 'non-cognitive' on the grounds that the latter is more cumbersome and implies a negativity which is inappropriate.

The tendency to divide psychological concepts into separate compartments, to dichotomize what are in fact continua, has been prevalent ever since psychology aspired to becoming a science. It is based probably on a laudable eagerness to quantify and to classify – since this is done in the more advanced, physical sciences – though, in my view, this is pushing psychology into running before it can walk, with the predictable result that it sometimes stumbles and sometimes goes backwards. Let us consider a few such dichotomies:

experimental psychologist / clinical psychologist; extraversion /

introversion; creativity/intelligence; behaviour/experience; group factors/specific factors; cognitive test/personality test.

If one visits a department of psychology in the U.S.A., whether for a day or a year, the first question one is liable to be asked is 'Are you an experimental or a clinical psychologist?' In England, where we are less forthright, the query may take the form, 'Are your interests mainly in the experimental or the clinical field?' Either way, the implication is the same: you cannot respectably cultivate both. If you protest a professional interest in both, you may become *persona non grata* with both sides. Mutual mistrust often obtains between the two. (The present writer found it almost impossible to remain a member of the relevant two lunch clubs, when in the United States, despite having innocently received an invitation from both.)

The clinical psychologist tends to regard the experimental psychologist as an impersonal, mathematically-minded robot, belonging to a highly specialized, narrow in-group, conducting with great expertise experiments which do not even aim to increase our understanding of functioning human beings. For this in-group, 'noise' has nothing to do with sound, 'information' has little to do with knowledge, 'communication' denotes a sophisticated form of non-communication and 'intelligence' can be applied as aptly to a machine as to a person, and more aptly to a machine than to a dog.

On the other hand, the experimental psychologist is apt to regard the clinical psychologist as woolly-minded, kind-hearted and rather gullible – as one who means well and who is deluded into believing that psychiatrists know their stuff and that psychometrists produce tools worth using.* The attitude of the head of a department of experimental psychology to a successful student who wants to do clinical psychology is analogous to the attitude of the head of a public school, a few decades ago, to a bright

---

*A psychometrist is someone who specializes in mental 'measurement'. He is usually a qualified psychologist and he concerns himself, typically, with the 'measurement' of such mental qualities as intelligence, aptitude, flexibility and introversion.

pupil who was not attracted to Classics, namely, 'It would be a pity to waste him' (i.e. a pity not to force him into Classics).

So the vicious spiral continues. The two stereotypes correspond more and more closely to two existing kinds of psychologist, and the schism between clinical and experimental psychology ever deepens. It is, of course, possible for the clinician to use experimental methods – as, indeed, he should – but this is rarely attempted and may incur discouraging comments from both sides.

The extraversion/introversion dichotomy is a very different affair but it is worth examining for its exemplification of the 'operational' approach [A]. One may hear a lecture, for instance, about extraverts and introverts and gain the impression that these are two diametrically opposed types of people, who tend to behave very differently in the same situation. If one then has the opportunity, and the temerity, to ask whether everybody fits into one or other of these groups, and whether such grouping has any diagnostic significance, the lecturer will probably explain (*a*) that he is using the two key words simply in terms of a particular set of test scores, ('operationism') (*b*) that these test scores yield a fairly symmetrical frequency distribution [B] and, therefore, (*c*) that he has used in his work only the top and bottom 10 per cent of the scorers, (*d*) that the 'diagnostic significance' consists of a correlation with the scores gained on another psychological test. He may be sufficiently operational (and honest) to add (*e*) that he is not interested in the question whether these test scores are related to any external, non-laboratory criterion [C].

There would be no objection to this arbitrary procedure if the researcher always made clear its arbitrariness and its ivory towerhood. But presumably if he did so, he would not have much of an audience since most people – if they are clear about it – are not greatly interested in learning simply how a small, atypical minority of scorers on one test performs on another test. So the parochial nature of the results must *not* be made clear; and terms *must* be used, such as 'extravert' and 'introvert', which do have some meaning for the man in the street, even if his meaning differs somewhat from that of the lecturer, and the lecturer's meaning differs again from that of a psychologist with a different set of tests. Here is plainly no genuine dichotomy.

Little time need be spent on the creativity/intelligence division, since it has some points in common with extraversion/introversion, and moreover this division is discussed at length in chapter 4. Here it suffices to say that there is little evidence, once again, of a true dichotomy either on the criterion of the tests used ('creativity' and 'intelligence' tests yielding a positive correlation) or on the more empirical criterion of real life. In general, highly creative people are well above average intelligence – though many highly intelligent people lack the creative impulse and gifts.

The opposition of behaviour and experience dates from J. B. Watson's 'naïve Behaviourism'[3] of the teenage years and early twenties of the twentieth century. The word 'naïve' is put in for the benefit of present-day behaviourists [D]. Contemporary psychologists, however, who are not behaviourists consider it naive to treat experience as unimportant and introspection as worthless. But the point here is the *separation* of behaviour from experience which is implied by those who say that Behaviour is the only legitimate subject matter of experimental psychology. That the two are merely two facets of the same process and, at some level, are known to be so is shown by such studies as research on dreaming (a highly subjective experience) by means of such (behavioural) cues as eye-movements, changes in respiration and research work using the electro-encephalogram.

It is true, of course, that people can lie and can be mistaken about themselves but this objection to introspection is double-edged for it is possible also to 'misbehave' – in the sense of giving false behavioural cues (not necessarily confined to speech and the voluntary muscles). The writer would suggest that behaviour and experience are so much integrated that to study either, in human psychology, whilst excluding or denying the other, is the height of naïveté. At present, there is a tendency for the experimental psychologist to study the former only and for the psychoanalyst to concern himself almost exclusively with the latter. There are exceptions and it is to be hoped that their number will grow.

The battle of 'group factors' versus 'specific factors' has been waged long and briskly in the history of psychometrics. There are even now some who feel strongly on the question. Tests have sprung up and flourished like dragons' teeth, regardless of the particular theory held on this count by their deviser. To those who are not deeply involved in the issue, it seems – as with so many psychological topics – not to be the case that either one is right or wrong. It surely is not a question of discovering 'the truth', since the truth is less clearcut than either theory. It may be more fun to come down firmly on one side or the other and to identify oneself with this or that giant of the past, that is, of the time when psychologists who disagreed did so with a vigour and dogmatic certainty which is rarer to-day. But, fun or not, the results of years of testing suggest that there is a strong common element in most cognitive tests – call it 'intelligence' or what you will – and that its strength and its type will vary, naturally enough, with the tests used. Similarly with the less common elements: they tend to cluster to a greater or lesser extent. There is no hard and fast answer to be found, either by means of purer (or coarser) tests or bigger and better statistics.

This brings us to our sixth and last example, the distinction between intelligence testing and personality testing. Since this topic constitutes the major part of the book and is discussed at length in several chapters, we shall be brief here. The distinction concerns that between the cognitive and the orectic which was outlined near the beginning of this chapter. Much used to be made of it when psychology was still a part of philosophy and it had a certain convenience at that time, when theorizing about human experience was *de rigueur*. Now, however, that the distinction is perpetuated in psychometrics, and the term 'personality test' by tacit consent means a test which cuts out the cognitive elements (as though this were possible), this is an affront to psychology, to common sense and to semantics. It is an *untenable* distinction and most of the rest of the book will be devoted to an attempt to demonstrate this.

2 Heredity times Environment

Water is H_2O, Hydrogen two parts, Oxygen one, but there is also a
third thing that makes it water, and nobody knows what that is –
D. H. LAWRENCE

Heredity times environment – Fallibility of tests – Meaning of
'intelligent'

Intelligence is the product of heredity and environment – some
would go so far as to say 'heredity four parts, environment one' [E]
– but as, Lawrence puts it, there is also a third thing which may,
for brevity, be called 'personality'. This quality too is the product
of heredity and environment and it is dealt with at some length
in chapters 6, 10 and 11.

Everyone would now agree that nature and nurture both play
their part in determining the degree of intelligence of an individual but, after this, agreement is at an end. What is interesting is
that the relative importance assigned to the two varies with the
political leanings of the psychologist drawing his conclusion.
The right-winger tends to emphasize the role of heredity whilst
the left-winger stresses the importance of environmental influences.
Both occasionally use information based on parents or siblings,
whereas the only acceptable data are those based on a comparison
between identical twins reared together and reared apart – of
whom there are but few.[1] As in other disciplines, since selection
of evidence is inevitable, both select and amplify that evidence
which best suits their book, to the virtual exclusion of less
amenable data.

Insofar as the nature/nurture question is meaningful with regard
to intelligence, it is primarily one for the geneticist. But the psychologist does have a contribution to make. He can emphasize the
fact of *interaction* between the two and of the occasional *inconstancy* of this interaction. He can indicate the complexity of
intelligence, underlining the fact that it is in no sense a simple

attribute (as those who draw the analogy between psychology and the physical sciences implicitly suggest). He can stress that heredity, at most, sets the upper limits. He can offer some help in the technique of appraising intelligence and he can – though he does not always – make it clear that his methods are sometimes fallible and never wholly accurate. As a theorist and a practitioner he should take every opportunity of affirming the necessity of a stimulating and sympathetic environment if the innate potential of the child and the adolescent is to be realized. This latter point bears the hallmark of experimental respectability since its truth has been demonstrated not only with children but also with rats[2] and other animals.[3]

Let us consider some of these points in greater detail. Psychologists who are concerned with the cognitive aspects of human beings seem to fall broadly into one of two categories. On the one hand there are those who treat intelligence as a unitary trait, valuably and straightforwardly measured by a reputable intelligence test. This is an extreme view, perhaps worth discussing. On the other hand, there are those who are so taken with the notion of creativity, *as opposed to* intelligence, that they overstate strongly in the other direction, throwing out several well-set-up toddlers with the bathwater. This topic also is an interesting one; it is discussed in Chapter 4.

However intelligence be defined, it is complex and not simple. This means that, genetically speaking, it is multiply determined and that psychologically speaking, its facets are many and varied. It is thus meaningless to speak, as many distinguished psychometrists do, of an individual's 'true intelligence' or 'true score'. And to make statistical calculations in order to approach more nearly to this hypothetical true intelligence is misleading as well as time-wasting.

To ask whether someone has (or has not) blue eyes is both meaningful and verifiable. To ask whether someone is (or is not) intelligent means little. To enquire what *degree* of intelligence he has is an improvement, but it still implies the existence of an attribute which differs simply in degree.[4] There is a tremendous urge at present to quantify. This urge is experienced not least by psychologists – but we seem to have forgotten the lesson of the earlier, natural history type of psychology that to quantify too early or too exactly, or to quantify in ignorance of what our figures mean, is worse than not to quantify at all. One and the same psychologist is quite capable of developing sophisticated techniques and making the complicated calculations required in order to ascertain the *g*-saturation or the construct validity (*see* Chapter 12) of an intelligence test and at the same time producing series of 'intelligence test' items which are wholly lacking in cogency (*see* Chapter 3). He who perpetrates such items must be unaware both of the logical requirements of a test problem and the psychological importance of the relation between test and Subject. It is vital that test items be both logically defensible and be seen to be so by those who take the test. Tacit, mutual contempt between tester and tested is all too frequent a phenomenon, despite lip-service routinely paid by the tester to the 'establishment of rapport' – as though this can be switched on and off at will.

It was said, above, that the psychologist can offer some help in the appraisal of intelligence and that he should make clear the fact that his methods are sometimes fallible and never wholly accurate. This caveat is appropriate even in the case of well-designed, carefully constructed tests which do not assume that their potential users are gullible and uncritical. The best of tests can never be 100 per cent accurate, partly because there is no such thing as a person's 'true intelligence': our moods vary and our moods affect our functioning intelligence – and some people's moods vary more frequently and violently than others. Moreover some people have brilliant but highly specialized mental ability. Such Subjects tend to do very well in their chosen intellectual field but relatively poorly in intelligence tests. This again is linked with their personality: they often show a characteristic kind of intellectual obstinacy, stubbornly failing to accept what may seem obvious in the problem not only to the test-deviser but also to the Subject who is more of an all-rounder.

Even if the claims of the psychometrist have often gone too far, it is still the case that a reputable test is the best single means of assessing an individual's intelligence, whatever definition (or lack of definition) is adopted. The intelligence test is more objective, more consistent, more valid as a first approximation than are any of the validatory criteria against which the test may be calibrated. This paradox underlies the whole mental testing movement. It is elaborated in Chapter 12.

It is now time to return to our quotation from D. H. Lawrence ... 'and nobody knows what that is'. We have established one sense in which nobody knows what 'intelligence' is, namely, that we have no satisfactory criterion against which to validate an intelligence test. There is also a second sense, namely, that psychologists continue to differ in their definitions of the word 'intelligence' and, in my view, this is not merely a matter of semantics. On the other hand, that there is some common element among the diversity seems clear from the fact that, firstly, intelligence tests tend to correlate with one another more highly than they do with other cognitive tests (such as spatial perception or mechanical aptitude), and, secondly, intelligence tests are found useful in practice by school teachers and other educationists, sociologists, vocational advisers, psychiatrists, G.P.s and others whose job it is to help, and to take decisions about, human beings. (Psychologists have purposely been omitted from this list as it might well be claimed that they have a vested interest in keeping intelligence testing alive.)

In general, the intelligence test score broadly accords with the other criteria and it is on this accordance that the claim for validity is based. But the intelligence test is most useful when it does *not* tally with the Subject's scholastic achievements or his career in early life; and especially when the discrepancy is *positive*, i.e. when he gains a higher test score than was to be expected. In such cases even if nobody knows what intelligence is, we may infer that the Subject has more of this quality than had been supposed and that he has been functioning below this capacity, very likely for emotional reasons. Every time this happens, we can find out a little more about 'what that is'.

On what then does the 'common element among the diversity' depend? Let us first look at a few of the many definitions and descriptions of intelligence that have been offered by psychologists.

Such offerings, and discussions on them, abound.[5] The best known is probably Burt's 'innate, general, cognitive ability'.[6] This definition is intended to cover 'intelligence' in both the laboratory and the non-laboratory situation. It has already been suggested above that 'innate' is an over-simplification, theoretically and practically [F]. The point may become clearer in the discussion of Hebb's definition which immediately follows. The remainder of Burt's definition is unexceptionable if one is prepared to 'define intelligence' (as opposed to *describing intelligent activity* – the present writer's preference) and to accept the cognitive/orectic dichotomy – which it is difficult to avoid in this context.

Hebb also tackles the problem of both 'intelligence-test performance and . . . any intelligent behaviour'.[7] In his chapter entitled 'The Growth and Decline of Intelligence', he writes as follows: '. . . it appears that the word "intelligence" has *two* valuable meanings. One is (*A*) an *innate potential*, the capacity for development, a fully innate property that amounts to the possession of a good brain and a good neural metabolism. The second is (*B*) the functioning of a brain in which development has gone on, determining an *average level of performance or comprehension* by the partly grown or mature person' (Hebb's italics throughout). He goes on to state that only intelligence *B* is influenced by experience and that, in his view, the disputes in the literature (over nature/nurture and definitions of intelligence) have arisen 'partly because of the double reference of the term "intelligence" . . .'

The present writer would disagree with the latter suggestion, believing that psychometrists and non-physiological psychologists would have little interest in the hypothetical intelligence *A*. Insofar as they accept the distinction, they have always concerned themselves with intelligence *B*. It is evident from most of Burt's writings that he is concerned with intelligence *B* and it seems to me that Hebb has put forward the idea of 'two different meanings of intelligence' in an endeavour to solve the 'innateness' problem to everybody's satisfaction. It neatly sidesteps the question but seems to do little more.

Intelligence has been defined, optimistically and circularly, as 'that which is tested by intelligence tests'. Miles maintains that this is not circular, 'if in the definiens we substitute the names of *particular* intelligence tests' (Miles's italics).[8] To me, this addition seems merely to decrease the circumference of the circle. To say that 'x is that which is tested by P's test of x' is surely as circular as to say that 'x is that which is tested by tests of x'. The former does give more information in that it tells the listener that P's test is considered to be a good one, but it does not fulfil the requirements of a satisfactory definition – namely, to explain the meaning of the crucial word, preferably so that someone unfamiliar with it can henceforward understand it and that an authority in the relevant field can accept it. Moreover such a 'definition' offends against the rule that the word to be defined should not itself appear in the definition. Thus this definition (which is not always given facetiously) is unsatisfactory on two counts. If it is considered in its most general form – as 'that which is tested by intelligence tests' – it is not even true, since there are a number of so-called intelligence tests which positively penalize the more intelligent Subject (*see* Chapter 3).

A still more lighthearted suggestion is that 'intelligence is that which allows us to do without education, and education is that which allows us to do without intelligence'. Two definitions for the price of one – and as usual in such circumstances, the wares are slightly substandard. There is a grain of truth in the remark but this grain was larger in the past than it is now. Fortunately, intelligence and education tend more and more to go hand in hand, as academic education becomes increasingly available to those who will enjoy it and profit from it. Children and adolescents of reasonably high intelligence rarely fail nowadays to be exposed to education; some of these people may lack the interest or temperament to get much out of it; and some with lower intelligence also have good educational opportunities and may fare better than had been predicted. As the sum total of human knowledge grows at an accelerating rate, however, it becomes harder and harder for the uneducated but intelligent to get by – and the number of those who do is probably dropping. On the other hand when one does, occasionally, come across the highly educated person without any great degree of intelligence, he tends to be a mine of factual information, with which he is disconcertingly ready to part. He usually, and understandably, strongly disapproves of psychological tests.

Let us now consider how the two best-known devisers of individual intelligence tests, Wechsler and Binet, claim that they use the term. Wechsler defines intelligence as 'the aggregate or global capacity of the individual to act purposefully, to think rationally, and to deal effectively with his environment'.[9] This definition confirms the 'generality' already noted in Burt's definition. It goes less far than Burt's 'innate' but it goes further than his 'cognitive', since this definition explicitly includes purposeful acting and effective dealing with the environment – in addition to rational thinking. Thus for Wechsler (writing in 1944) intelligence was conative as well as cognitive and, in his individual tests, whether for adults or children, he has ranged over as wide a field as it is possible to do without exhausting the Subjects. His intelligence tests have stood the great test of time, as have those of Binet, who was constructing intelligence tests and writing about them at the beginning of the twentieth century.[10]

Binet was less willing to give a straightforward definition of the word. He wrote 'It seems to us that in intelligence there is a fundamental faculty, the impairment* or lack of which, is of the utmost importance for practical life. This faculty is called judgment, otherwise called good sense, practical sense, initiative, the faculty of adapting one's self to circumstances. To judge well, to comprehend well, to reason well, these are the essential activities of intelligence.'

In spite of his declining to give a definition, Binet has told us a great deal. He evidently considered intelligence to be general and not specific, to include conation as well as cognition. His canvas was vastly broader than that of his successor and developer, Terman, who wrote (in 1921) that 'an individual is intelligent in proportion as he is able to carry on abstract thinking'.[11] Whilst

*This word is normally mistranslated into English as 'alteration' – the French word being '*alteration*' (= impairment or deterioration).

this is true, it is surely insufficient. For Binet, intelligent behaviour included 'practical sense, initiative, the faculty of adapting one's self to circumstances'. None of this *need* be related to abstract problems although of course it may, on occasion, be so.

Binet's work, too, has stood the test of time. His writings, though forty years earlier than Wechsler's have not dated. His tests have been refined and amplified but not radically changed. Various additions have been made, including the extension of his scale to Subjects over fifteen and under five years of age. It is questionable, however, whether the latter addition is wholly satisfactory, in view of their relatively poor validity and consistency: correlations between the test results of two-, three- and four-year-old children and the results of the same children at a later age are so low as to be of doubtful value.

One criticism of Binet that should perhaps be made is his adoption of chronological age (or, rather, of what-the-child-can-do-at-what-age) as his criterion of intelligence. He was probably right to base his famous intelligence scale on this, as it is external to the tests and wholly objective. But it seems to have escaped his notice that *whatever* is being tested tends to improve with age between five and fifteen – be it performance on a general problem of reasoning, a highly specific mechanical or spatial task or a physical, athletic task. Thus improvement with age is no guarantee that it is necessarily intelligence which is being assessed. This criticism applies to his theory rather than his practice, for most of his tests were conspicuously well-chosen for their purpose.

Innumerable definitions of intelligence have been offered by psychologists since Binet. As the mental testing movement grows and intelligence tests proliferate, yet another schism seems to be developing. On one side stand the operationists who tend to confine themselves, more or less explicitly, to intelligence as tested. The others are in the unfortunate position of being forced to do the splits: they stand with one foot on either side of the widening gap, endeavouring to achieve a definition, or at least a description, which will include intelligence as tested and also as understood by the layman. For this purpose, the description of intelligent activity which I offered some years back may perhaps be acceptable. 'Intelligent activity consists in grasping the essentials in a situation and responding appropriately to them'.[12]

This is a description of intelligent activity, not a definition of intelligence, since I do not wish to perpetuate the notion of an isolable entity called 'intelligence'. It implies that there is a sense in which one's behaviour can be, intellectually, less (or more) than worthy of oneself. This is in line with the approach of experience-cum-behaviour and personality-including-intelligence which is advocated in this book. It deliberately leaves open the question whether the more intelligent person is he who can solve the most varied problems or he who can solve the problem posing the greatest difficulty. It is intended to apply equally to intelligent activity as displayed when taking an intelligence test or a non-cognitive test, and as displayed in real life. In Chapters 5, 8 and 9, an attempt is made to outline the best method of appraising this elusive and complex quality, by means of tests.

3 Assets and Drawbacks of Multiple-choice Questions

'A hair, they say, divides the false and true' – OMAR KHAYYÁM

Advantages and drawbacks of multiple-choice questions –
Examples of unsound items – The importance of cogency

Group intelligence tests are usually in the form of multiple-choice items [G]. This device eliminates the demands made on the Subject in a conventional examination that he should write consecutively and at speed. Many examination candidates complain, with or without justification, that they are at a disadvantage in that they write slowly and cannot get their thoughts on to paper in the time allowed. There are, of course, educationists who think it highly desirable to ascertain whether the candidate can express himself with intelligible fluency and these can always set an academic examination or an essay, in addition to a psychological test. Indeed, an intelligence test, administered with any practical aim in mind, should never be given in isolation.

Apart from abolishing the effects of speed of writing, multiple-choice questions have the advantage of being swift, and wholly objective, to score. (They can, moreover, be arranged in such a way as to allow of machine scoring.) With this advantage, however, goes the drawback of requiring the test *problems* as well as their answers, to be wholly objective. This means that questions involving judgement or personal opinion of any kind must be excluded and that only problems which can and do have one single correct solution may be used.

Thus, degrees of rightness (and of wrongness) are eliminated, at least in theory. In practice, as is inevitable, some of the incorrect solutions are closer to correctness than are others and, moreover, some are more attractive-looking than others. But the aim is a series of questions with only one logically defensible answer. This is clearly very unlike the problems which are encountered in everyday life, where there are relatively few clear-cut

29

problems with clear-cut answers. In most real-life situations – and in almost all situations of interest – judgement and taste play a large part in determining the line to follow; the solution is often a compromise or a choice of the least of several evils.

Multiple-choice, then, imposes an artificiality and a rigidity on the test items which is perhaps compensated for by the objectivity of the resulting test – when it *is* objective. If, however, the test items are not cogent, if they reflect too strongly the particular biases and prejudices of their deviser, then the test may antagonize its Subjects and mislead its users. The more difficult the test is designed to be, the harder it is to achieve items which fulfil the condition of cogency – and the more important this condition is, since the Subjects taking high-grade tests are more critical and capable of making finer discriminations than are less intelligent people.

In many intelligence tests currently used, the 'hair dividing the false from the true' is so fine that it is invisible save in the eye of the test-maker. The purpose of this chapter is to give illustrations of some of the unsound items and to demonstrate the damage which may result from such lack of soundness. The examples which follow are drawn from several tests, all devised by big names in psychology. It has not been necessary to delve into obscure byways to find them. All the items come from published tests whose devisers are household names in psychometrics.

Let us first consider the type of problem generally known as Classification, for items of this kind are particularly fallible. The Subject is presented usually with five or six words (or they may be numbers, diagrams or pictures) and is asked to indicate which one is in a different category from the others. The instructions are not identical from test to test: one may ask for the 'odd man out', another for the member which 'does not belong', but the meaning is usually clear. The solution, however, is sometimes far from clear.

captain   frustrate   house   labour   swing

This question may look at first cogent and even interesting, in that it is somewhat out of the ordinary run of Classification items. A little thought reveals that four of the words are used as both nouns and verbs whereas one, 'frustrate', is usable as a verb only. Is there anything against this solution? – apparently not, if the answer is assumed to relate to the meaning or function of the five words. Reference to the marking key, however, reveals that the author of the test had in mind the *number of vowels* in each word. He, therefore, claims 'swing' as the correct solution – this being the only word which contains only one vowel, as opposed to three vowels in each of the other four words – and, moreover, he remains adamant that 'swing' is the only correct answer, 'the only one which takes into account all the data'. A case can, of course, be made for 'swing' (as, indeed, can for 'labour' – the only word comprising an even number of letters) but since at least as good a case can be made for 'frustrate', the whole problem lacks cogency. It is worthwhile stressing again that the highly intelligent Subject is at a disadvantage here because he is likely to perceive two answers (or more) and he will be penalized if he gives the 'wrong' one or if he gives more than one.

Fresh from consideration of this Classification item, let us inspect one which consists of only four words:

courage   leave   measles   steamer

After the last one, this looks easy. One can see at a glance that each of the last three words contains three vowels and those three are identical vowels, presented in the same order – e, a, e. 'Courage' contains four vowels, two of which do not occur in the other stimulus words. So we settle for 'courage'. But, before turning to the key for confirmation, we suddenly realize that three of the words comprise two syllables and that 'leave' is the only monosyllabic word of the four. Moreover 'leave' is the only word which can be used as a verb as well as a noun. So with *two* reasons for 'leave' we turn hopefully to the key. Here, however, we find 'steamer' given as the answer for the following reason: 'The other three words are colloquially connected with three nationalities – Dutch courage, French leave, German measles; steamer is not.'

Again, consider:

animal   engine   identity   octagon   unicorn

Here the solution is claimed to be 'unicorn' (not because it is the only mythical beast, but) because 'in all the other words the first and last vowels are identical'. This is, in fact, not true of the word 'identity' (whose y is used as a vowel) – and which might, incidentally, be taken as the answer since it is the only abstract noun.

This type of difficulty may be thought to be specially characteristic of *verbal* Classification items since words contain letters – few and many, curved and straight and mixed, vowels and consonants – and the words themselves are often rich in ambiguities and associations. But similar objections arise in Classification items whose terms are numbers. We are asked, for instance, which [one] of the following numbers does not belong with the others.

625   361   256   197   144

We can quickly reject the concept of simple odd/even, since there is more than one of each. The numbers are rather large: let us try adding their digits together. This gives us 13, 10, 13, 17 and 9. Ah, of course! The answer must be 361 as this number is the only one whose digits add up to an even number. But are they not all factorizable, except 197? Yes, this is the case. So this question has two possible answers. Let us consult the marking key. This gives 197 'because all the others are squares'. Here then we have a new phenomenon – the possibility of giving the right answer for the wrong reason.

Another numerical question, in a different form:

'Insert the missing number'. The answer and explanation given are as follows: '32. Multiply the first number by the second to get the third: $1 \times 2 = 2$; then multiply the second and third numbers to get the fourth, and so on. $4 \times 8 = 32$, so that 32 is the missing number.' This is certainly one way of looking at it. One could, however, say with equal cogency: 'Consider each sector and its opposite number. Thus $1 \to 4$ (1 multiplied by $4 = 4$); $2 \to 8$ (2 multiplied by $4 = 8$); therefore $2 \to$ blank (2 multiplied by $4 = 8$); therefore blank $= 8$'. The answer is then, defensibly, 8. There is also a third possibility if the figure be taken to incorporate two series. The first would go: 1, 2 (i.e., the *second* 2), 8 – the reasoning being $1 \times 2 = 2$ and $2 \times 4 = 8$. The second series would go: 2 (i.e. the *first* 2), 4, blank – the reasoning being $2 \times 2 = 4$ and $4 \times 4 = 16$. The answer is then, defensibly, 16.

Lest the assumption of two series in one be thought to be farfetched and improbable, let us consider the following question:

Insert the number which completes the series

$$7 \qquad 9 \qquad 40 \qquad 74 \qquad 1526$$

Here the answer and explanation are as follows. '5436. There are two series, beginning respectively with 7 and 9, and going on to alternate numbers. For the one series, square 7 and subtract the figure immediately following 7, i.e.; $7^2 - 9 = 40$. Similarly, $40^2 - 74 = 1526$. For the other series, square 9 and subtract the figure immediately before 9, i.e. 7; $9^2 - 7 = 74$. To get the missing number, square 74 and subtract 40; this gives 5436.' Not only is this far-fetched and improbable but the wording, 'insert the number' is misleading, since it suggests that the answer should come somewhere between the first and the last of the given numbers. Moreover the data are inadequate.

Let us now consider a horse of another colour, coming from a different stable. This time the question requires the Subject to select from five words one which means *the same* as the first word in the sentence.

Blend means the same as . . . mix, combine, mingle, confuse, add.

The solution to this question provided in the marking key is 'combine'. Reference to a dictionary, however, reveals that 'to blend' means, among other things, 'to mix, to mingle'. This

33

again is a problem which lacks cogency, owing to the fact that more than one of the solutions provided (in this case, three) are defensible. Such questions lack the objectivity which is part of the *raison d'être* of multiple-choice items. They are indeed highly subjective, since they depend directly on the state of mind of their inventor at the time he devised them.

Similar snags easily arise in word-making. For example:

B (. . .) OW

Insert the word that completes the first word and starts the second.

One can offer B(END)OW, the two words being 'bend' and 'endow' or one can equally cheerfully offer B(ALL)OW, the two words being 'ball' and 'allow'. There are probably others which fit equally well.

In the illustrations so far given, there have always been two or more candidates for the correct answer. In the two that follow, however, there seem to be no right answers at all.

Victim is the opposite of ... hunter, happy man, imposter, benefactor, cad

According to the marking key of this test, the answer is 'benefactor'. This is pure nonsense. 'Victim' is no more the opposite of 'benefactor' than it is of 'hunter', 'imposter' or 'happy man'. Finally:

Wait is to Event as Fall is to ... Slip, Weight, Push, Water, Obstacle.

No answer suitable – or even, possible.

A good many examples have been given of unsound test items because they turn up with alarming frequency and the matter is thought to be important, by the Subjects who take the tests and by the present writer. This view is evidently not shared by the perpetrators of such items since they tend either to deny the lack of cogency or the importance of the matter. One may read, for instance, in the Introduction to MENSA that they 'have discovered in [their tests] a number of doubtful questions ... but that they are quite satisfied that they do not invalidate the results of the tests as a whole'. This seems hardly good enough for an organization whose sole condition of membership is exceptionally high intelligence, as tested, and whose President is Sir Cyril Burt. If some questions in their tests are thought to be 'doubtful' (as indeed they are) this surely throws some doubt on the tests which include these items and, hence, on the results of the tests.

There are three points to be considered here: the attitude of the people being tested, the validity of a test which includes invalid items, and the whole theory underlying the practice of mental testing. There probably will always be some Subjects who are dissatisfied after taking an intelligence test, but there should never be any whose dissatisfaction is *justified* on the grounds of shoddy questions. One poor item in a test can undermine a Subject's belief in the value of intelligence testing (and some tests contain far more than one such item) and psychologists should not be complacent about the attitude of Subjects to tests.

Certain testers take a lofty, contemptuous view of their Subjects, analogous perhaps to the contempt felt by some motorists for pedestrians: they are slow, they talk another and an inferior language, they are downright inconvenient – but we cannot do without them. Such motorists forget that we are all pedestrians and that the car was invented for the benefit of the pedestrian. The contemptuous mental tester, who no doubt regards himself as highly intelligent, is being foolish in not realizing that his Subjects will grow up to be parents and educationists and politicians. They simply do not accept his assurance that, as an expert in the field, he knows best and has only to reiterate his correctness more loudly in order to prove his point. Sometimes, as shown above, they are quite right to disbelieve him. In any case, the psychologist of all people should recognize others as human beings – as ends in themselves and never just as means to his ends. In view of his subject-matter he should remain upright (if not fall over backwards) in his endeavour to be and to appear correct and just. The same point applies to those experimental psychologists who think they can manipulate their groups of Subjects, for instance, by telling members of this group that they have done very well and telling members of that group that they have failed badly — regardless of the actual performance of the group-members [H]. This is foolish as well as unethical. It is absurd, psychologically, to expect people who have performed a task well and were told that they failed to have the same experience, and hence display the same behaviour, as people who performed the task poorly and were told that they failed.

The hair dividing the false and true in intelligence test items, then, should be strong and thick, partly in order to avoid an undesirable attitude on the part of the Subject. Also, as mentioned above, there is the validity of the specific test and the whole basis of the mental testing movement to be considered. If the inclusion of a doubtful item in a test 'does not invalidate the test as a whole', the item must, at best, be valueless. A test does not exist apart from its items; it is made up of them. Psychometrists spend much time and thought on methods of item analysis[1] and usually insist on a certain minimum positive correlation between each item and every other [I]. This is scarcely consistent with the admission of worthless or doubful items.

Finally, such doubt strikes at the root of the theory and practice of mental testing. The psychometrist needs not only to scrutinize his every item in the severest possible way, he should behave as though a test is as strong as its weakest item. There are many psychological theories about intelligence and its testing,[2] and the majority of these are closely linked with the results of intelligence tests. Thus, if any constituent part of a test is invalid, this invalidity is liable to be reflected in the whole theory, whatever it may be, on which the testing is allegedly based. The external criteria for intelligence test validation are admittedly unsatisfactory (*see* Chapter 12). The internal criteria derive directly from the results of the tests (factor analysis [J], construct validation [T] etc.) There is no certainty that these are right even if the tests on which they are based are good, but there is reason to think that they are wrong if the tests on which they are based are in any way unsound.

4 Creativity and 'Creativity'

I will not Reason and Compare; my business is to Create –
WILLIAM BLAKE

*Creativity and ' creativity' – ' High creative/low I.Q.' and ' high
I.Q./low creative' – Convergence and divergence – Arts
and science*

So far, I have mainly discussed multiple-choice questions. The
thinking involved in such questions is 'tied' rather than 'free' (*see*
quotation heading of Chapter 5) since the answer is confined to a
choice of five or six solutions, sometimes, lamentably, fewer. In
addition, as we saw in Chapter 3, the deviser of such tests has
tacitly to agree to limit himself in the subject-matter, as well as in
the form, of the problem. According to the quotation heading
given at the beginning of Chapter 5, such questions do not stimu-
late or require genuine thinking. This may be thought to be
going a little far – yet judging from the writings of some of the
psychologists currently interested in Creativity, it is scarcely an
overstatement.

The notion that mental Creativity is a vital human attribute is
not new. Trying to *test* for Creativity is considerably newer, but
even this is at least two decades old. It was in 1950 that Guilford,[1]
in his presidential address to the American Psychological Association, deplored the lack of interest shown by psychologists
in creative ability as compared with their continuing devotion to
the study of intelligence and its testing. He recommended the
initiation of research into the possibility of developing tests of
Creativity along factor analytical lines, such tests, naturally, to be
open-ended [G].

Since then, 'creativity testing' has got going in a big way and
has repeatedly hit the headlines. It has done so, partly because of
a reaction in some quarters against the I.Q. and the 11+ and
much that intelligence testing is thought to stand for, and partly

because the Creativity merchants – and some have indeed been peddling their wares – have made some extravagant and eye-catching claims.

The literature in this field is large and swiftly growing.[2] In general, however, a fair measure of agreement obtains on the type of test used and the type of conclusion reached. Let us first consider the former of these. The tests used which are largely verbal, include

(*a*) 'Uses for things'. In this test the Subject is asked to think up as many different uses as he can for common objects, such as a brick, a blanket, a paper clip. This test derives from one originally devised by Guilford,[3] in his factor analytical work on cognitive ability.

(*b*) Word associations. The Subject is presented with ambiguous words, such as 'fair', 'bolt', and is asked for as many meanings as he can think of for each word.

(*c*) Fables. In this test, the Subject is asked to make up three different endings for fables, the last line of which is missing. One ending is required to be 'moralistic', another 'humorous' and another 'sad'.

(*d*) Problem-devising. Here the Subject is presented with a long paragraph containing many numerical statements. His task is to produce as many mathematical problems as possible, based on the data given in the paragraph. This type of test is, clearly, not exclusively verbal.

There are two further tests worth mentioning here, both with a visual bias. One

(*e*) Consists of asking the Subject for a drawing, in response to a given title, such as Playing Tag in the School Yard. The other

(*f*), Hidden Shapes originally devised by Gottschaldt, is one of Cattell's 'Objective-Analytic' Tests. It consists of simple geometric shapes each of which is followed by four complex figures.[4] The Subject is asked to find which one of the complex figures contains the simple geometric shape.

There are other 'creativity tests' but these are sufficiently representative to illustrate the approach. It will be seen that all but (*f*) have a high degree of open-endedness and, again with the same exception, that they are not intended to have correct or incorrect answers. The greater the number of answers given and the greater their variety, the more highly will the Subject score. This has the advantage of allowing free rein to the imagination and the fluency of the Subject. It carries with it the drawback that far-fetched, bizarre, and even psychotic, answers may score highly – if this is a drawback. The scoring, inevitably, is less objective than in multiple-choice problems. For instance, the decision as to whether a self-styled 'humorous' ending to a given fable is, in fact, humorous or not depends on the sense of humour of the test-scorer.

The users of these tests are not at first dogmatic as to whether what the tests assess is the same as that usually designated as Creativity. They take, very reasonably, as their starting-point the view that the concept of 'intelligence' has been overstressed, that this may have blinded us to the potential ability of the individual whose gifts do not lie in his I.Q. and that these tests, being different in kind from traditional cognitive tests, may prove indicative of the more elusive, fluid, real life attributes which are variously called creativity or originality or constructive imagination.

What then of the extravagant and eye-catching claims, mentioned above? These relate to the type of conclusion reached by some 'creativity testing' enthusiasts. It is claimed, for instance, that there is a substantial minority of individuals (*a*) 'who are high on creativity and low on I.Q.' and (*b*) another minority consisting of those 'high I.Q. and low on creativity'; that there is a tendency for the former, at school and later, to go on to the Arts side and for the latter to go on to the Science side; that the former are liable to be 'divergers' and the latter to be 'convergers'.

Let us consider these various points in turn. Our text will be mainly Getzels and Jackson's *Creativity and Intelligence*, as this is one of the studies from which others have stemmed and it is highly relevant to the present purpose. This book is based on the alleged distinction between (*a*) exclusive high creativity and (*b*) exclusive high intelligence, mentioned in the preceding paragraph, despite the following facts: That the 450 adolescents tested by Getzels and Jackson were all intellectually very able, being drawn from a private school of high academic standing, and having a mean I.Q. of 132; that the Creativity tests and the I.Q. tests correlated positively and significantly; and that, therefore, in order to attain their (a) and (b) groups, Getzels and Jackson were forced to take children who came in *the top 20* per cent on one criterion (summated Creativity scores, or I.Q.) and in *the bottom 80* per cent on the other criterion (I.Q. or summated Creativity scores). Even so, this yielded only 26 boys and girls for the 'high creativity, "low" I.Q. groups' and 28 for the 'high I.Q., "low" Creativity group'. Those Subjects who scored highly on both measures were ignored. Note that the high scorers on both counts plus the low scorers on both counts constitute 88 per cent of the total group.

The conclusions drawn from this study were numerous and often stimulating but they were largely vitiated by the selectiveness of the main group and of the sub-groups chosen for investigation, and the neglect of the authors to study the children who scored highly on both measures. The latter Subjects would have provided a larger and less artificial sample than the two sub-groups around whom the book was written. To take one example: Getzels and Jackson found that the 'high creativity, low I.Q.' child was less approved of by school staff than was the 'high I.Q., low creativity' child. They go on to suggest from this finding that teachers are perhaps wary of the creative child, as such. But Hasan and Butcher, in an excellent 'Partial replication with Scottish children of Getzels and Jackson's study' show that this is not the case.[5] Hasan and Butcher find that children who are high on both measures receive still higher ratings from school teachers, on desirability as a pupil, than do the 'high I.Q., low creativity' pupils. In fact this brief paper, by studying the child who is high on both measures, instead of ignoring him, solves a good many of the more superficial problems raised by Getzels and Jackson's book and perpetuated by their followers.

What of the second, widely publicized claim, that the (a) 'high creativity, low I.Q.' child tends to gravitate towards the arts and the (b) 'high I.Q., low creativity' child, towards the sciences? It is surely true that, given the artificial dichotomy already described, the (a) child is more likely to specialize in modern languages, history and English and the (b) child in physics, mathematics or engineering. (Hudson,[6] who is very keen on this idea, has discovered that for his purpose classics is a science but that chemistry, and also biology, are non-sciences.) Is this direction of specialization unexpected? Clearly not. But is it based, as suggested by some Creativists, on the hidebound rigidity and the fusty matter-of-factness of science as she is taught, thus frightening away the more enterprising and imaginative adolescent? This is certainly not the full explanation; in fact, it is probably a very small part of it.

Acceptance of this explanation would suggest that the 'creativity tests' are indeed testing creativity, which is still open to question. This is not merely a semantic matter nor is it irrelevant to the arts/science problem. Constructive creativity may well demand the fluency and imaginativeness required by many of the tests but it demands also some degree of self-criticism and judgement. If we consider the Uses for Things test, for instance, it is likely that a fair number of the Subjects who think of 'breaking a window' as a use for a brick, censor this. Such a Subject will do less well on the test than will the uninhibited answerer who does not hesitate – but the former Subject, who both had the idea and decided to drop it, may well prove to be the better scientist. A further objection to the 'creativity tests' is that they concern themselves solely with fluency and novelty and ignore the question of the *urge* to create – which is, perhaps, the most distinctive feature of the genuine (non-divine) creator, be he successful or unsuccessful.

Again, the explanation offered in terms of the dullness of science teaching ignores the important subgroup, whose members do well on both types of test, and who would probably be found to divide themselves roughly equally between the arts and the sciences, however defined.

Lastly this explanation, in common with much of the work on

creativity, neglects intellectual capacity at the expense of intellectual interest (closely related though these two usually are). It is probable that those few 'high creativity' adolescents who have a low I.Q. – absolutely, as opposed to relatively – would simply be unable to cope with scientific subjects, if they tried. There are many different qualities of mind and the typical scientific mind is essentially that which is good at deductive reasoning and attention to detail (both assessed by intelligence tests). Whereas the type of mind of the successful artsman is essentially the fluent, free-associating, intuitive mind (assessed by creativity tests). No doubt teaching methods in science (as in arts) subjects can and should be improved; steps are already being taken in that direction.[7] But if the (a) children are attracted by the humanities and the (b) children by science and mathematics, this is largely because their gifts and their interests go hand in hand. The few children who are genuinely 'high creative, low I.Q.' would be miserable failures if they took up science.

This brings us to the third claim: that the future artsman tends to be 'divergent' and the future scientist tends to be 'convergent' – or, rather, that the diverger is pushed and pulled towards arts specialization whilst the converger drearily accepts the grey hand which draws him into science specialization – and hence, that many lively minds are lost to science. The terms 'divergent' and 'convergent' thinking have undergone several changes of dress since Guilford coined the terms.[1] They are now used to mean different things at different times.

First, and perhaps most frequently, 'convergent/divergent' is used to designate the distinction between multiple-choice and open-ended problems. Thus, any question which supplies solutions (even if it concerns artistic preference, as do the items in the Meier Art Judgement test[8]) would be 'convergent', whilst any question for which the Subject is requested to produce his own answer would be 'divergent', however cut-and-dried and unique the required response to the latter may be. But, secondly, the terms are sometimes used to denote the difference between problems which have a correct answer, as opposed to those which do not have a correct answer. In this sense, open-ended analogies, vocabulary and series problems, for example, would be designated as convergent and only those problems which cannot by their very nature elicit any 'wrong' responses would be called 'divergent'.

Confusion, so far, is twofold: (a) because the key words refer to different distinctions and (b) because some writers implicitly suppose that the one equals the other, i.e. that a problem which is convergent in the first sense will necessarily be convergent also in the second sense. A third source of confusion lies in the fact that the terms are sometimes used to connote a *type of problem* and sometimes to connote a *type of person*. This leads us to the third use of 'convergent/divergent', that which applies exclusively to people.

The psychologists in question write (generally in somewhat pitying, condescending tones) of 'convergent people' and (generally in approving, admiring tones) of 'divergent people'. One student having listened, sceptically, to a lecture along these lines came out saying, 'It's the baddies and the goodies, all over again!' He spoke, perhaps, more wisely than he realized. An individual described as 'convergent' is, by implication, good at walking, blinkered and unquestioningly, along a prescribed groove; it is understood that the groove is narrow, arbitrary and leads, if anywhere, to somewhere dull. On the other hand, the person described as 'divergent', it is suggested, is lively, enterprising and free-ranging in exciting, unexplored territory.

The mistake is sometimes made here, by the over-enthusiastic, that since the creative person is often unconventional and contrasuggestible, the unconventional and contra-suggestible are necessarily creative. This is an error both in elementary logic and in empirical observation. Divergence, as applied to people, carries with it the further implication that they may well be nonconforming and aggressive – if not, indeed, downright sadistic. They may also, of course, be expected to fare worse than the 'convergers' on multiple-choice tests and/or on tests for which correct solutions exist.

It seems a little much to require the same pair of words to carry all three of these connotations. And, should the Creativity testers protest that the three go together in practice, even if the three *meanings* are admitted to be distinct, this too is unproved and likely to be unprovable in view of the positive correlation found, though often ignored, between the convergent and the divergent tests (in the first two senses).

These criticisms need raising but, in our view, the moral is by no means that 'creativity testing' should be lessened in scope. It is rather, firstly, that those concerned with 'creativity testing' should be more cautious in their interpretation of test scores and their choice of Subjects, and more generous in extending examination of their test results to include the high scorers on both measures; and secondly, that it is worthwhile considering the psychological test which is both 'divergent', in the sense of open-ended, and 'convergent' in the sense that correct answers exist for it and are known. These latter tests combine the main advantage of 'convergent items' (objective scoring) with many advantages of 'divergent items' (the Subject produces his own responses, thus enabling him to demonstrate his fluency and ingenuity, and *degrees of correctness* can be allowed for). Such tests were foreshadowed in *The Appraisal of Intelligence*,[9] since when a few have been devised. These are discussed in the next chapter.

5 Open-ended Tests with Correct Solutions

All thought is free or it is no thought – MOLIÈRE

Correct solution in open-ended tests – The Word-in-context –
The Self-judging Vocabulary Test

This chapter is concerned with cognitive tests which are open-ended but for which correct solutions (and, therefore, incorrect solutions, also) exist. The argument will be easier to follow if it is based on actual tests, and the two tests dealt with are the Word-in-context[1] and the Self-judging Vocabulary Scale.[2] This choice may seem somewhat egocentric since both of these are tests for which I have been responsible. However, it is precisely on account of familiarity with the tests and the type of results they yield, that they have been chosen. Non-cognitive tests (which may be open-ended or closed) whose answers are generally intended to be 'neither right nor wrong', are considered in Chapters 10 and 11.

The Word-in-context (Winc for short) was devised for some of the same reasons that prompted the construction of Creativity tests. Its authors felt that the traditional intelligence test, as it became increasingly 'pure' over the decades, became also increasingly artifical and narrow; that its validation methods have become increasingly inbred, (notes [A] and [J]); that its application is very limited in the case of older people and psychiatric patients; that its items are often monotonous or far-fetched or both; and that it damagingly perpetuates the myth of separability between the cognitive and the orectic aspects of mental life.[3] The authors of the Winc were aware that certain projective techniques, such as the Rorschach[4] do set out to assess both temperament and intellectual calibre. But, apart from the fact that these tests are time-consuming to give and subjective in interpretation, the notions of *correctness* and *incorrectness* of response scarcely apply. Such tests, therefore, convey at best a general idea of the

Subject's intellectual level: they cannot yield much that is quantifiable or usable for purposes of comparison.

For these reasons, then, the Winc was developed. Intended primarily to be a group test of general reasoning with a verbal bias, it is believed to differ from other such tests in the following respects:

(*i*) It provides a test situation which is similar to, if not identical with, a frequently-met real life situation.

(*ii*) It requires inductive reasoning from the Subject, in addition to deductive reasoning.

(*iii*) It is objectively scorable in the sense that a correct answer exists for each problem. It has the advantages, however, of being 'creative answer' in form and also of allowing for *degrees* of rightness (and wrongness).

(*iv*) It does not seek to isolate the cognitive aspects, in the way that has become customary. In addition to its assessment of reasoning ability the test may yield data concerning certain orectic traits, such as flexibility and conscientiousness.

(*v*) There are grounds for hoping that the Winc may prove to be a useful tool in research on thought processes, in particular on concept formation, and also in clinical work with older people and deteriorated patients.[7c]

The Winc test is in two parts. First the Subject is given a list of words each of which he is asked to mark as *a* or *b* or *c*. *a* signifies: 'I know this word and could explain it to someone unfamiliar with it.' *b* is a broad category indicating doubt. *c* signifies: 'I have never seen this word before and have no idea what it means.' If a Subject raises difficulties or demands a further intermediate category, he is reminded: 'When in doubt, use *b*.'

Having marked the words *a*, *b* or *c*, the Subject is given a set of contexts for the words he categorized as *c*. Each set consists of three typed contexts (one context per sheet), presented in *descending* order of difficulty. The Subject reads the first context (*P*) – the most difficult of the three – and writes down the meaning of the word, in so far as he can interpret it from its context. He then does the same for the second (*Q*), easier, and for the third (*R*), easiest, context. He may interpret the word on its second appearance in the light of his present and previous evidence; and on its third appearance he has the benefit of the preceding two contexts. At the end, he may reread all three passages and then he is asked to give a final verdict on the meaning of the word. It is the 'final verdict' scores which are used as the test of verbal reasoning. The rationale of calling this process 'inductive' should now be clearer. It is hoped, too, that the answers to the separate word-in-contexts, P, Q and R, may yield data concerning such temperament traits as flexibility, conscientiousness and willingness to commit oneself on inadequate data.

The words in the list are selected from the prose works of reputable authors, British, American and South African. Many of the words, however, are obscure, archaic, dialect, slang or of foreign origin [K]. These have been included in order to ensure enough c words for such Subjects as modern linguists, classicists and specialists in Anglo-Saxon. An effort is made to ensure that all the words in the passages, apart from the crucial test word, are well known to the Subject. Each of the three passages is culled from a different writer. Below each passage is given the name of the author, the publisher, the book or periodical and also the date of publication. The original works are for the most part novels, biography, travel or articles on current affairs. Technical and scientific writing is excluded, as is poetry and translation. The average length per context is a quarter to a third of a quarto sheet of typescript and the crucial word usually occurs about the middle of the context. (*See* note [K] for illustrations of Winc contexts and scoring.)

The final verdict is scored on an 8-point scale. The three-context sets have proved difficult enough to yield a wide variety of final verdicts, even from university students. There is, however, some uniformity among the diversity, thus enabling a reasonably consistent system of scoring to emerge. This ranges from -2, the score for a wholly mistaken interpretation, to $+5$, an interpretation which is correct and complete.

The reasons for choosing 'real words in real contexts' are that these, unlike psychologist-made words,[5] have roots and carry conviction; that the lack of association value claimed in the early days for nonsense syllables has been disproved;[6] and that the crucial word, in the Winc passages, is the one which was chosen by the authors of the books from which the passages are drawn. They presumably selected it on account of its look, rhythm and flavour, in addition to its meaning. This important aspect of living language would be lost if anything but real words were used.

In addition, the variety of matter and style ensured by selecting three different authors for each set of contexts, wherever possible, was thought likely to enhance the interest and motivation of the Subject. In the event, this proved to be justified: 'It makes you want to read the whole book!' is a not uncommon reaction to some of the contexts. Finally, it was felt that the use of passages drawn from published books and articles renders the test situation less artificial. The technique used is merely an extension of the way in which everybody acquires new words from infancy onwards – by hearing or seeing unknown words, repeatedly, in different intelligible contexts.

A few experiments with the Winc test have been conducted[7] and many more remain to be done. At this stage, however, it may be said that the test effects differentiation among members of groups as varied as fourth-form school children, naval ratings and undergraduates; that its scoring allows for varying degrees of correctness, objectively determined; that, whilst correlating positively with (*i*) a vocabulary test and (*ii*) a non-verbal intelligence test, it appears to be assessing something different from both of these; that, unlike most traditional tests of intelligence, it does not favour the scientist and mathematician. There is also some evidence that the Winc correlates with academic examination in certain arts subjects, such as English.

In general, then, it seems possible to construct cognitive tests which are scored less subjectively and arbitrarily than are 'creativity tests', and elicit from the Subject higher motivation than does the traditional intelligence test. Such a test would be equally applicable to artsman and scientist, though there is some evidence suggesting that it might aid in differentiating the one from the other,[8] where the individual is in doubt. Owing to the freedom allowed the Subject in his form of response, it is conceivable that the test would yield data on some of the qualities of mind which interest the 'creativist'.

The second test to be dealt with in this chapter is very different in that it is a test of knowledge, rather than reasoning; artsmen tend to score significantly more highly on it than do scientists; and it is open-ended or multiple-choice or both, according to the wish of the Subject. We are most interested in the first of these points here, but we shall start by outlining the test and then briefly discuss the second two points.

The test is the Self-judging Vocabulary Scale (SJ for short).[2] This scale consists of five sets of forty words, named respectively A, E, I, O and U. A is the easiest, E is slightly harder, I is medium in difficulty, O is harder and U consists of extremely difficult and obscure words. The words *in each set*, however, are of roughly equal difficulty: there is little overlap, for instance, between the difficulty of those set O words which are comparatively hard and those set U words which are comparatively easy. This was empirically determined at an early stage. Each complete test comprises eighty words, made up of two adjacent sets. For example, 12- and 13-year-old school children would take AE; adults who left school at 15 or earlier would take EI; sixthformers would take IO; university graduates would take OU.

The test is conducted in two parts. The Subjects are first presented with their list of eighty words. These are arranged alphabetically in ten columns of eight words. The Subjects are instructed to *a/b/c* the words in the same way as they are asked at the beginning of the Word-in-context. As each Subject finishes, his list is removed and he is handed Part II of the test. This consists of a booklet with the same words in the same order, but after each word there are printed six phrases: the Subject is instructed to select the phrase which best corresponds to the stimulus word. The following examples give some idea of the clarity of the task, the variation in the stimulus words and the difference in difficulty levels of the five sets. It will be seen that the correct answer is not always *a definition* of the word – nor is it so described in the test instructions.

exhibit (level A)

1 put on one side
2 boast
3 forbid
4 show
5 correct a fault
6 send out of the country

insulator (level E)

1 consultant
2 inhabitant of an island
3 go-between
4 higher civil servant
5 one who gives offence
6 non-conductor

recondite (level I)

1 cave-dweller
2 explosive
3 profound
4 seasoning
5 explored
6 foreseen

eschatological (level O)

1 hidden
2 theological term
3 wearing fur
4 obscene
5 fearful of shut-in-places
6 feline

strubag (level U)

1 makeshift mattress
2 horse's nosebag
3 slut
4 country bumpkin
5 prolonged snack
6 bundle of washing

In an attempt to minimize the inevitable advantage enjoyed by, for instance, the modern linguist and the classicist, as in the Winc some dialect and some words of foreign origin are included, but all the stimulus words have been encountered in reading British and American literature. Care was taken to include some words with a faintly scientific flavour, such as 'insulator' (given above), 'cumulus', 'vernier', in order that the early science specialist should not be unduly penalized. Despite this effort, however, scientists do fare far less well than artsmen on this test, at all ages where the Subjects have specialized.

The Subject is invited to give a seventh answer in his own words if he knows the crucial word but dislikes all the solutions offered. This was included in the instructions in order to reduce the discomfort of the occasional purist who might feel that, for some of the words he knows, none of the proffered solutions really meets the case. Such a Subject will indeed avail himself of the opportunity and turn the test, to some extent, into an open-ended one. But, interestingly enough, the giving of seventh answers is not confined to Subjects who know the crucial word. Surprisingly often, *incorrect* seventh answers are given – sometimes to words which the Subject had marked as *b*, or even *c*.

This illustrates the advantages of allowing a choice of mode of response, and demonstrates once again the intimate link between the cognitive and the orectic. The choice made as to whether to select from the six proffered phrases or to answer 'creatively' is surely at least as much a matter of temperament as it is of intellect. Equally clearly, temperament traits play a part in determining the proportion of *a*'s correctly answered. This varies tremendously. Few Subjects score 100 per cent on their *a* words, some score as low as 60 or even 50 per cent on them. This proportion has been found to vary with the total score: there is a tendency for people with high vocabulary scores to gain a higher percentage of correct *a* words than do people with lower vocabulary scores. Here again is the inextricable intermingling and interaction of the cognitive and the orectic. A final example is the absolute number of words marked *a*, *b* and *c* in the first part of the test. Some Subjects seem loth, for instance, to mark words as *b*. These may be 'intolerant of ambiguity', to use Frenkel-Brunswik's concept.[9] Others (with, perhaps, a comparable vocabulary) mark many more words as *b* being less willing, possibly, to commit themselves or being more 'tolerant of ambiguity'.

The SJ Vocabulary Scale differs from other vocabulary tests, then, in its combination of multiple-choice with open-endedness. This combined form might be useful in other tests where an objectively correct answer exists but where the tester would nonetheless welcome criticism and originality on the part of the Subject. This Scale differs, too, in having *no gradient of difficulty* within each test (although the steps are fairly definite between adjacent pairs of tests comprising the total Scale). The lack of difficulty-gradient results in these tests being tests of word-knowledge exclusively: they are less highly correlated with intelligence test scores than are vocabulary tests with a built-in-gradient.

In the light of the two tests described in this chapter, we can now consider the whole question of objectively scorable tests which are open-ended – or, as in the case of the SJ Vocabulary, are as open-ended as the Subject chooses. This element of choice, we would suggest, is in itself an invitation to the original and the critical Subject: it allows for a 'freedom of thought' which is not open to him in the exclusively multiple-choice situation. It has been shown (Chapter 4) that the divergent/convergent dichotomy breaks down, whether applied to tests or to people. Degrees of rightness are not catered for in the Vocabulary test but eight degrees are allowed for in the Word-in-context and are generally made use of. This is a long overdue departure from the over-simplified, right/wrong assumptions made in the traditional cognitive group test.

The most important innovation, however, is the explicit recognition of the inseparability of all aspects of personality:* the deliberate linking of the intellectual with the orectic in the form of the test questions and the system of scoring. This is quite different from the inferring of temperament traits from tests designed as intelligence tests.[10] It may be thought by some to be a retrograde step, since the measurement of intelligence has been claimed to be getting more and more pure, and more and more accurate, over the years. In a sense it is a backward step, in that this integration was clearly seen by earlier psychologists, such as William James and Binet. But it is also forward-looking, in the sense that it points to the living human being and recognizes his right to thinking and feeling, in addition to behaving.

*The very meaning of the word 'personality' as used by psychometrists underlines the point being made. 'Personality test' connotes a test of the non-intellectual aspects of the Subject. It includes such characteristics as extraversion and tendermindedness but usually excludes intelligence.

6 Meanings of 'Personality'

Grant but as many sorts of mind as moss – ALEXANDER POPE

*Meanings of 'personality' – Unacceptable distinctions between
cognitive tests and 'personality tests' – The role of motivation
and emotion in intelligent activity – Adaptation to level of difficulty*

The word 'personality', like 'intelligence', is one of those many
words which is used both by the layman and the psychologist.
For the layman the term is vague, and for the psychologist it is
ambiguous; but there is usually a certain overlap among the
various meanings. Without having recourse to Allport's mam-
moth work on Personality,[1] we can needle out three connotations,
of which two would be acceptable to the psychologist and the
layman. The first of these (*a*) is the whole human being, the
(non-arithmetic) total of all the characteristics which give him his
individuality and distinguishes him as a person, identifiably
different from all other persons. Just as everyone's handwriting
differs from everyone else's, so does his personality.

One might describe personality, in this sense, as the combination of all the traits, sentiments, aptitudes, prejudices, emotions,
attitudes, moods, self-perceptions, abilities, interests, skills,
recollections, desires, ambitions and manners which make up the
individual. This list is not complete: it could be added to almost
indefinitely. But the description is reasonably clear and suffers
only from the objection that it may suggest some atomistic theory
of personality. Since in my view a 'theory of personality' is not
practicable, I certainly do not intend to put one forward – least of
all an atomistic one – for, insofar as this book has a thesis, it is
the essential oneness of the human being. This phrase denotes
nothing mystical and nothing necessarily integrated. It is all too
clear that one can be a person and be dramatically disintegrated.
Such disintegration, however, would be an important feature of
one's personality, in this sense.

(b) The second meaning of personality as sometimes understood by psychologists and laymen is what might be called the 'shop-window' aspect of the person: that which strikes others about him at a first meeting, what he 'is like', superficially. Personality, in this sense, is of course a part of personality in sense (a). It is largely made up of appearance and manner and such qualities as shyness, charm and social dominance. In this sense, John Smith's friends may say of him: 'Don't be put off by John's personality. He is kind and thoughtful for others and very amusing, when you get to know him – not at all as he strikes you at a first meeting. He just has an unfortunate personality.'

This is obviously a very different meaning from the first one. Smith's personality in sense (a) attracts liking and respect, and his personality in sense (b) is unattractive and dislikeable. He is the kind of person who has loyal and loving friends and retains them throughout his life. But he takes longer than most people to make friends, because the contents and presentation of his shop-window are at variance with the excellent wares within.

These two senses, then, are accepted by the psychologist and by the man in the street. But (c) the third sense of personality – the sense taken by the psychometrist – is, understandably, not acceptable to the layman. This is the sense in which the word 'test' usually follows the word 'personality'. Interestingly enough, a so-called 'personality test' or 'inventory' is generally one which does not set out to assess either personality (a) or personality (b). It unashamedly aims to assess the orectic characteristics – the non-cognitive, non-intellectual aspects of a person – only.

Such tests used to be called tests of 'temperament and character'. They were no more successful in their aims than are contemporary 'personality tests',[2] but at least their blanket title was less misleading. The current terminology suggests that personality has little or nothing to do with the intellect: that personality is concerned only with such attributes as sociability, stability, cheerfulness, diligence, emotionality, selfishness, honesty, etc. Lest it be thought that an exaggerated picture is being drawn here of the psychometrist-made split between intellect and feeling, let us quote a very apposite statement from a couple of highly reputable psychometrists, Hathaway and McKinley, on one of the best-known and most used of 'personality tests', the Minnesota Multiphasic Personality Inventory.[3]

Personality testing can never yield scores with stability comparable to that of aptitude and interest scores. A test giving stable scores would probably be clinically of little use, at least for certain types of evaluation, no matter how valid it might be[*sic.* Indeed it is tempting to say *sic humour!*] With future research, it is not unlikely that we shall find a hierarchy of stability for various personality traits, some remaining quite constant, others being exceedingly variable.

This is quoted, not because of the paradoxical remark on validation (which confirms what is said in Chapter 12 about the confusion reigning over the concept of validation, owing to the all-embracing 'operationism' of psychometrists). Nor is it quoted because of the statement of the inherent inconsistency (lack of 'stability') of orectic tests. This is true and probably inevitable – though it seems a pity to employ the word 'stability', since this term is conveniently used to refer to people rather than tests: either 'consistency' or the more usual 'reliability' would be clearer here.[4] The passage is quoted because it shows so clearly the schism between 'personality' and 'the rest'. Here it is contrasted not merely with intelligence (though this is understood) but with aptitude *and interest* (my italics). The erosion grows apace! If this psychometric whittling away from the concept of personality continues at the present rate, it may soon be left with only 'neuroticism' and 'introversion/extraversion'. And then we shall eventually be told that 'personality' can be reduced to these two factors (*see* p. 88).

This is the point that is perhaps most worrying about psychological terminology: that an ordinary non-technical word is sometimes taken, precisely because research is required on that which is customarily denoted by it. The word is then pruned and groomed for scientific purposes, and – having been used in experiments in its new technical narrow sense – is then allowed to slip back into its non-technical, wider sense, complete with an experimental proof which does not belong with this non-technical sense. One is reminded of the days when it was stated that men could not suffer from hysteria, since 'hystera' means 'womb' and men do not have wombs.

The term 'personality test', then, is by psychometric consent a test which is not concerned with intelligence or aptitude. The briefest way to interpret the term is to explain that it applies to orectic characteristics exclusively. Thus any cognitive aspect of the individual is by implication irrelevant to his personality. He may be an absent-minded and egocentric genius but his genius, being a cognitive matter, has nothing to do with his personality! He may be a frustrated, border-line mentally defective school child, but his low intelligence is, for the psychometrist, evidently not part of his personality. He may have an average, run-of-the-mill intellect – apart, say, from an outstanding memory for facts – but be ruthlessly ambitious and self-seeking: the personality test may cover his ambition, self-seekingness and other temperament traits, but it is not concerned with his degree of intellectual calibre or his unusual powers of recall.

The absurdity of this terminology is clear to the layman – or, rather, psychological jargon is often baffling to the layman because of the latter's common sense and interest in human nature. The clinical psychologist and the educational psychologist who use the tests know perfectly well that they have to consider the child or adult as a whole: that his individuality depends on the interplay of his cognitive and his orectic attributes: that even this understates the case, since it implies differentiation between the two. Such psychologists have an important, often urgent, job to do and they use whatever tools are at hand, whatever these may be called – intelligence tests, aptitude tests, creativity tests, personality tests.

The omission of the cognitive element from 'personality tests' is, then to be deplored. It is felt to be a misuse of the word 'personality' and to play a strong role in maintaining the factor-analytical myth that people are composed of discrete, separable, measurable factors.[5] But there is also the other facet: the isolation of intelligence as tested (or g) from the non-cognitive aspects of human nature. And, of course, from 'intelligence as tested', it is but a small step to 'intelligence'. Hence the implication (when it is not actually stated) in psychometric text-books, that functioning intelligence is unaffected by mood, attitude, temperament, character, or aspirations.

Let us first consult with Smith's friend, Brown. He may say: 'I was so angry that I couldn't think straight'; or 'When my wife gets into one of her states, she doesn't know what she is doing'; or 'If my son hadn't *wanted* so much to get through, his teachers say he could easily have passed. He was too keen and he kept looking for catches that weren't there'; and 'It's just the other way with my daughter – she doesn't really care. But when she is interested, she does very well'; or 'The trouble with my nephew is that he's a perfectionist: he will not go on to the next task until he has checked and double-checked the last one.'

Surely it is common knowledge that strong emotions (not only anger) are usually incompatible with clear, logical thinking. When the emotion is at its height, one is apt to speak or act foolishly; when it begins to wane, one may have the sense to say 'I'll wait until I have calmed down' or 'I had better sleep on it' before giving an answer or reaching a decision. Surely it is common knowledge, too, that when one is in a neurotic state (and few of us have not so been, at one time or another) one behaves stupidly and maladaptively. It is easy to see the parallel, in simpler form with the unfortunate animals who have had experimental neuroses induced: cats, for instance, who refuse to eat when hungry and presented with food,[6] rats who continue repeatedly to jump at the right-hand opening, despite food being visibly available through the left-hand opening.[7]

Brown is right again when he blames over- and undermotivation for displays of behaviour which are unintelligent. Living beings respond best to the essentials in a situation when they are interested in what they are doing and are keen to attain the relevant end – but not too desperately keen. Both excessive and insufficient motivation may reduce our functioning intelligence. The last example given by Brown is that of his nephew. It is true that if he is a perfectionist, obsessively determined to achieve 100 per cent accuracy at the expense of whatever speed, he will act apparently unintelligently in many situations (though not, of course, in all). But, as in all these examples, it is not *intelligence* that is lacking. It is the result of anger or neurosis or inappropriate motivation or obsessionality, interacting with the individual's cognitive abilities and reducing them. Brown and his friends know these facts of life from observation and introspection. The experimental psychologist, as he moves ever further from human beings and is thus increasingly able to over-simplify psychologically, may ignore these facts or their relevance. Or he may take refuge in the difficulty of quantifying them.

It is true that experiments on humans in this border zone are scant compared with the vast numbers conducted with rats, but there are a few which may relevantly be quoted here. Bruner and Goodman, for instance, have shown how the perception and judgement of children vary with the wealth of their parents.[8] In this experiment (subsequently repeated and confirmed by Carter and Schooler[9]) three groups of 10-year-olds were tested, individually, on their ability to reproduce the size of a coin, which they had just been shown. The three groups were, respectively, from well-to-do homes, from poor homes and from varied economic backgrounds. Coins of five denominations were used. The coins of higher denomination tended to be overestimated by all to a relatively greater extent than were coins of lower denomination. But the overestimation of large coins was greater by the children of poor parents than it was by the children of rich parents. It was inferred that judgements of size were being influenced by judgements of value and desirability.

We would stress here the importance of accurate perception and judgement for an intelligent response, whatever the situation. Such accuracy, is not, of course, *sufficient* for the Subject to act intelligently, but it is *necessary*. The work of Heckhausen on the effect of achievement motivation on performance in various tasks is also relevant here.[10]

Again, Helson has shown in a variety of situations how adaptation to intensity of stimulus alters the degree of correctness of the response.[11] This has also been shown by Mace, who found that when an easy and a difficult version of the same task was presented to equated groups of Subjects, the harder version generally evoked a better performance than did the easier version.[12] This held with tasks as varied as dart-throwing and arithmetical computing, and seemed to be the result of manipulating the Subjects' motivation and their adaptation level.[13]

All the studies so far quoted illustrate the inseparability of the capacity of the Subject on the one hand (accuracy of perception, judgement, sensori-motor co-ordination, simple calculations) and his orectic aspects on the other (feelings about value and desirability, motivation, level of aspiration). Since, however, we are primarily concerned in this book with intelligence and its appraisal, let us consider an experiment in which adaptation to level of difficulty was shown directly to affect the functioning intellectual level of the Subject.[14]

In this experiment two pairs of tests were prepared using a selection of items from one high-grade and one easier intelligence test. The four tests comprised the same number of questions but they differed in their number of 'difficult' problems and in their time limits, the harder tests being allotted proportionately longer time limits. A group of Subjects was selected, given a preliminary, standard test of intelligence and, on the basis of their performance, divided into four equated subgroups. Each of these subgroups took one or other pair of 'mixed' tests in one or other order. Thus identical problems were presented, in contexts of varying degrees of difficulty, to equated Subjects.

The main results were as follows.

(a) Evidence of *immediate* adaptation to level of difficulty was found when a comparison was made of the scores gained on difficult questions in an easy context and a difficult context, respectively. The mean score on the difficult items was found to bear a statistically significant relationship to the proportion of difficult to easy items in the test: the more numerous the harder questions, the higher their mean score. Moreover, identical difficult problems were solved more often (by equated Subjects) when they appeared in their harder context.

(b) The data suggested also the operation of *successive* adaptation to level of difficulty. Subjects taking first the easier test of the pair gave evidence of some downward adaptation, achieving fewer correct solutions to the difficult problems in their (harder) second session than did members of the equated group when taking this (hard) test for the first time. Similarly, upward adaptation was demonstrated by those who took first their more difficult test: these Subjects showed greater accuracy per question on the difficult problems in their (easier) second session than did equated Subjects taking this (easy) test first.

(c) The time limit imposed on the test taken first appeared to influence the speed with which Subjects tackled their second test. Those whose first test was easy, and therefore short, worked faster, attempting a greater number of items, in their second test (although it was more difficult); whereas those whose first test was hard, and therefore long, worked more slowly on their second test (although it was easier). This last finding reflects also on the inadequacy of a simple 'speed/power' dichotomy, favoured by certain psychometrists.[15] This latter topic is highly relevant to that of personality but it is discussed in Chapter 9.

Thus both 'upward adaptation' and 'downward adaptation' may occur in intelligence testing, although the Subject is unaware of it. A similar phenomenon was demonstrated in an experiment on adaptation to level of difficulty in judging the familiarity of words.[16] This, again, was a cognitive test but it concerned knowledge, and self-estimates of knowledge, rather than reasoning.

The relative paucity of studies of this kind is readily understandable. Such experiments would be conducted in the main by psychometrists and, if later results confirmed the earlier ones quoted above, they would undermine much that has long been assumed by psychometry. Such assumptions include, for instance, that it is possible to use one intelligence scale along which the total population can be distributed; this would ignore the 'downward adaptation' of the high scorers and the 'upward adaptation' of the lower scorers (though it is unlikely that those right at the bottom would show this).[17] A second assumption is that a Subject's response to the same test problems is constant. The results of the adaptation work suggest that the Subject's ability is not necessarily absolute, that he may not only do himself *less* than justice sometimes (a contingency which is recognized by some psychometrists) but that he may – given a sufficiently extending test context – sometimes do 'surprisingly well'. It looks as though we may be on the way to an explanation of these phenomena – as opposed merely to designating such Subjects, with faint disapproval, as 'under-achievers' and 'over-achievers', respectively.

A third assumption concerns 'objectively based' levels of difficulty of particular problems. It now looks as though this concept has less generality than was previously thought.

The main practical lesson to be learned is the importance firstly of determining the *relationship* between level of test and level of Subject (seen also in the chapter on practice effects) and secondly of paying more than lip-service to the role of affective and attitudinal factors, and also to the role of instructions, in cognitive testing.

7 The Influence of Practice on Test Performance

Practice is better than Precept

The influence of practice on test performance – Coaching,
practice and discussion of errors – Test-taking as a skill

During the early years of the second world war, a psychological
joke was going the rounds of Departments of Psychology. It
went something like this: Sergeant says to his Commanding
Officer, 'I don't think much of those tests you told me to give the
men. I've been giving them once a week for months now and
they're not showing any improvement.' Mirthful collapse of
stout psychologist hearing the story – because he knows that what
the tests measure is innate and therefore not susceptible to
practice effects. Naturally no improvement will be found: that is
the whole point of the tests.

We have come a long way since then. It is now publicly acknow-
ledged that environment generally plays an important role in
test results and that practice, in particular, does have a marked
effect on the scores of psychological tests. Many schools, somewhat misguidedly, have introduced psychological testing into
their weekly curriculum, having at heart either the good of the
child or the glory of the school, in the educational rat race. Many
experiments have been conducted on the effects of practice in
mental testing. In 1953–4, the *British Journal of Educational
Psychology* published a Symposium on the Effects of Coaching
and Practice in Tests.[1]

Thus it is clear that psychometrists agree that practice does
influence test performance. The agreement goes further than this
general statement, however. First, it has been found that by far
the most striking effects occur during the first few practice periods.
This is why the introduction of a weekly exercise in test-taking
over a term or more is described above as 'misguided'. If such
periods are continued for too long, the Subject is apt to become

stale, to lose his freshness and whatever degree of interest he may have had to begin with. It is easy and rather depressing to gain a *déjà vu* effect from taking countless intelligence tests, with the result that the Subject is tempted to make the occasional risky snap judgement. He may say to himself, 'Oh, that's like the question we had last week so *this* must be the answer.' Had he come fresh to the problem, he might have taken the trouble to work out the answer from scratch and he might not have made the snap judgement – with its error.

Secondly, there is agreement that the shorter the time-interval between test and retest, the greater the improvement on retesting tends to be. Retesting (whether on the identical test or a parallel test) after one week, for instance, usually produces a greater increase in scores than does retesting after, say, six months. Two reservations should, however, be made: (*a*) if the second test be taken immediately after the first, fatigue effects may overcome practice effects; (*b*) if the interval is longer than a few months, and the Subject is under about sixteen years of age, it may be difficult to distinguish between the effects of practice and those of maturation.[2]

Thirdly, as might be expected, the greater the similarity between one test and the next – in form, medium and subject-matter – the greater the increase in score. Thus the improvement found, for instance, when a test of verbal reasoning, in one particular form, follows a test of verbal reasoning in the same form, is far greater than when a diagrammatically biased test follows a verbal or a 'mixed' test. Fourthly, considerable individual differences have been found among Subjects with respect both to their susceptibility to practice effects and their 'coachability'. It is generally agreed that some Subjects profit more than others from practice and that certain Subjects benefit from coaching on tests to a much greater extent than others.

After this, however, the agreement on the effects of practice and coaching in mental testing is at an end. Some psychometrists claim that coaching has more effect than practice[3]; some claim that practice has more effect than coaching.[4] Some find that the brighter Subjects (initially higher scorers) tend to show the most improvement[5] and others find that the duller Subjects (initially lower scorers) tend to show more.[6] Yet others find no relationship between practice effects and level of ability.[7] Vernon suggests that the inconsistency found among the results of different investigators may be due to 'methodological problems: the large Standard Error (or unreliability) of coaching gains, the expression of gains in non-comparable units, and the failure to control the difficulties of tests that are being compared.'[8]

These factors do surely contribute to the apparently chaotic results. But, in my opinion, two additional circumstances may also play a part. (*a*) The conflicting practice/coaching results may be due, it is thought, to certain differences in usage of the key terms, 'practice' and 'coaching'. (*b*) Conflicting findings as to whether the initially high scorers profit more (or less) from experience of tests than do the initially low scorers, may be due to the tendency of psychometrists to think in terms of absolute test difficulty and absolute Subject's ability, instead of in terms of the all-important *relationship* between the two. Let us look at these two points in some detail.

(*a*) Some of the earlier investigators have attempted to differentiate between 'practice without coaching' and 'coaching without practice'. The latter phrase seems to the writer to be self-contradictory. If there is no practice there can be no coaching, as the term is usually understood. Moreover it was not always made clear whether the 'coaching' included that vital teaching aid, 'discussion of errors'. Lastly several of the reports on relevant experiments stated apologetically, at some stage, that the tests were found not to be strictly parallel. This, of course, renders evaluation of the results difficult, if not impossible.

For these reasons, Heim and Watts conducted an experiment on Practice, Coaching and Discussion of Errors in Mental Testing in which they used (spatial) tests which had been designed to be strictly parallel.[9] Spatial, as opposed to intelligence, tests were chosen because seven of these (Shapes Analysis[10]) tests were available, their level of difficulty L having previously been equated, on the two criteria of proportion of Subjects responding correctly and of time taken per question.[11]

The Influence of Practice on Test Performance

In this experiment, the effects of practice on identical tests was examined in addition to the effects of practice on parallel tests (as well as the effects of coaching, with and without discussion of errors). The tests were administered weekly to thirteen- and fourteen-year-olds, drawn from six schools: two secondary modern girls', two secondary modern boys', one central girls' and one boys' grammar. On the basis of the first test score, every form was divided into five equated subgroups, each of which subsequently received different treatment. Two subgroups took the *same* test (Test 1) for six consecutive weeks, one of these subgroups receiving coaching but not the other. The remaining three subgroups took a *different* (parallel) test each week, receiving between sessions either coaching, or discussion of the previous week's errors, or neither. At the final session, every subgroup took Test 7. 'Coaching' here signifies explanation and discussion of the principles used in the Shapes Analysis test, by means of items which were similar to, but not identical with, the items given in the experimental tests.

Thus, 'coaching', 'practice' and 'discussion of errors' were fairly clearly differentiated, the coaching involving some degree of practice but the practice involving no coaching. Practice on the *same* test was distinguished from practice on *similar, parallel* tests. No knowledge of test score was given to individuals during the course of the experiment.

These experimental results too were not unequivocal, mainly owing to the fact that inter-school differences equalled or exceeded inter-subgroup differences. The following conclusions could, however, be tentatively drawn. Discussion of errors is the most effective improver of performance on a *new* test. Coaching plus practice is more efficacious than practice alone, whether the practice task be the retaking of identical or of parallel tests. Coaching plus practice-on-the-same-test produces better performance on a new test than does practice alone on different tests. Practice alone on the same test yields the poorest result, on the criterion of performance on a new test. Differences in temperament among individuals and groups were found to contribute materially to the results.

One further series of experiments is worth quoting, this time on tests of intelligence.[12] In this series, the Subjects took the same test once a week for ten weeks (in some cases, less). They were given no coaching, no discussion of errors and no knowledge of individual results. The reason for selecting this particular study is that by means of using two intelligence tests of different level,[13] and four different groups of Subjects, the investigators were able to experiment with the relationships between group-level and test-level. It was this juggling with the relationship that differentiated this research from others on the question of practice effects and that helped to reconcile the hitherto conflicting results as to which Subjects tend to profit most from practice.

The four groups of Subjects in this series of experiments were as follows: (i) W.E.A. students with an age-range of 21 to 54; (ii) high-grade mentally defective schoolboys between 14 and 16 years of age; (iii) Naval Ratings, aged 18 to 20 years, most of whom had left school at 14; and (iv) students from the Cambridgeshire Technical College evening classes, with an age-range of 18 to 45 years. The first two groups took, as their weekly test, AH4; the second two groups took AH5, a much harder test. Thus a bright group and a dull group took the easier test; and an average group and a bright group took the harder test. AH4 was easy, on the whole, for the W.E.A. students but was very difficult for the high grade mentally defective schoolboys. AH5 was difficult for the Naval Ratings but was within the scope of most of the Technical College evening students.

For the present purposes, five main conclusions may be selected. (a) Whilst it was true for all the groups that the greatest mean improvement occurred at the beginning of the test series, a slight rise in score was still observable in the later weeks, save in the case of the W.E.A. students on AH4 – who by this time were encountering an artificial ceiling, i.e. many of them were attempting all the questions and gaining nearly 100 per cent on what they attempted. But (b) even though the test was on the easy side for this group, especially after several weeks of it, nobody did in fact gain 100 per cent. This links with what is said in Chapter 6 about 'downward adaptation to level of difficulty'.

(*c*) Test consistency was high within the four groups over the series of testings. Product moment correlations [1] were calculated between every pair of testings, for each of the groups. With the exception of one pair (second testing with seventh testing in the mentally defective group), *r* in every case exceeded 0·8 and in most cases exceeded 0·9. This suggests that the effects of individual variation – within groups whose members are equally test-sophisticated – are surprisingly small. The least consistent of the four was the group of mental defectives. This is probably due to the combination of their low intelligence (which resulted in their answering being nearly random) and their temperamental lack of stability.

(*d*) It was found that the duller Subjects showed most improvement on the visually biased (diagrammatic) items. This finding confirms the suggestion made in Chapter 7 that it is desirable to incorporate as many biases as possible when constructing an intelligence test. This is especially important in work with Subjects of low intelligence who may have had varying amounts of practice in taking tests.

(*e*) The problem of whether the brighter or duller Subject profits more from practice begins to look soluble. The conflicting results obtained by previous research workers are probably explained by the fact that many tests do not fully extend all members of a group after several testings and that investigators have tended to take a 'static' rather than an 'interactive' view of their tests and of their Subjects. Examination of the four experiments jointly, suggests that when the test is easy for Subjects, the initially lower scorers tend to improve most, as they have most scope: the higher scorers reach their artificial ceiling comparatively early. When, however, the test is difficult in relation to the Subjects (as it was for Groups (*ii*) and (*iii*)), then the initially higher scorers tend to improve most: no artificial ceiling depresses their later scores. One may generalize then to the extent of saying that *given comparable opportunity*, Subjects with initially higher scores will tend to improve more than those with initially lower scores. It is not known whether these results would apply to longer-term experiments with longer time-intervals between testings, or to experiments in which parallel tests were used instead of identical tests. But the results seem to make quite good psychological sense.

To sum up, the analogy between test-taking and acquiring a 'skill' is perhaps closer than has been realized by psychometrists. They resemble one another in several ways: practice produces an improvement in all Subjects whose level of ability is roughly suited to the level of the test. (If the test level is far too high or far too low for the Subject, improvement is unlikely to occur – just as, in comparable circumstances, a skill is unlikely to be acquired.) In both, a plateau tends to be established after some periods of practice. In both, an understanding of the relevant principles, and of the probable causes of error, achieves a greater advance than does mere mechanical repetition.

Part of the rationale of intelligence testing is that individuals vary tremendously in their capacity for tackling a test – both initially and after practice. This is true and, as we have seen, their *relative* capacity remains virtually unchanged if all are exposed to an equal amount of practice. This too tends to be true in acquiring skills such as playing cricket or the violin, for instance. Just as some people 'will never learn' to play either of these with conviction and enjoyment, however much they practise, so some people 'will never learn' to shine in an intelligence test. And just as the cricketers and violinists who become outstanding are in general those who start off pretty well, so the test-sophisticated Subjects who score most highly tend to be those who begin well – provided that they have *sufficient scope* for improvement.

In addition to these similarities, however, there are differences between acquiring a skill in the accepted sense and reaching a plateau on an intelligence test. For one thing, the would-be learner of violin-playing (or cricket, or computer-programming) usually makes further progress when he reaches the end of his first plateau, if he continues to practise. In such skills, this is often the shape:

The learner, on reaching the end of the plateau E F may effect a further rise, F G.

This may or may not be gentler in slope than D E (as is the case in the diagram) and it is often followed by a further plateau – in this case, G H. In test-taking, the Subject is unlikely to rise above the E F level, however much he practises.

One last difference lies in the *specificity* of conventional skills. Cricket and violin-playing are both highly specific – though there may be some transfer effects to ball games and music-making, respectively. Every skill is specific to a greater or lesser degree, whereas, as we have seen, intelligence testing is concerned with *general* ability. But, general or specific, there is in the acquiring of all techniques a strong constitutional element and a limit beyond which even the most appropriately motivated cannot hope to go.

8 The Need for Variety among Intelligence Test Items

... compounded of many simples, extracted from many objects –
SHAKESPEARE

The need for variety among intelligence test items –
Importance of preliminary examples

'He'd be good at intelligence tests: he has a crossword puzzle mind' (disapproving school teacher). 'My wife got a first in physics at Oxford but her I.Q. came out at 104 – two points lower than mine' (meek chemistry professor). 'Does the intelligence tester think he is brighter than all the people who are going to take his ruddy tests?' (angry young man). 'I suppose these tests are all right for children but some of them are terribly boring for older people' (sceptical parent).

Anyone who works in the mental testing field will be familiar with strictures of this kind and could add to them almost indefinitely. Most people have encountered intelligence tests at one or other stage of their lives – either directly or through their children – and most seem to hold strong views on the subject. In the writer's opinion a well-constructed test can be a valuable instrument, useful from both a theoretical and a practical viewpoint, and sometimes indispensable, if social and educational justice is to be done. Yet there is a grain of truth in some of the caustic comments quoted in the preceding paragraph.

Certain intelligence tests do indeed resemble crossword puzzles in that they are exclusively verbal, they demand acquired knowledge rather than logical reasoning, and they require experience of the particular quirks of the test-deviser. It is generally accepted that Smith is a '*Daily Telegraph* man' whereas Brown is a devotee of *The Times* crossword. Neither the newspapers nor the crossword competitors see anything shameful in this nor would they wish to deny their high degree of specialization. But when it comes to an intelligence test, the Subject will get nowhere if he pleads that he is a Cattellian as opposed to an Eysenckist! And all test constructors apparently believe that they have achieved ultimate truth and complete objectivity, even if they are developing their tests under great pressure and at high speed. They forget that they, like the constructors of crosswords, are human.

Such tests, however, are poor tests – as was the one on which the chemistry professor and his wife (they do exist) gained I.Q.s of 106 and 104, respectively. He was resigned about it, partly because he and his wife had done outstandingly well academically, and partly because he felt, as he said, that the tests they had tried 'were evidently measuring intelligence in some special sense – something we don't seem to have much of '. He assumed, however, that all intelligence tests were pretty similar.

This takes us to the third reflection in the opening paragraph of this chapter. Evidently many test-devisors do think that they are brighter than their potential Subjects – and also than their psychological colleagues – since they obviously do not seek their aid when developing a test. A new intelligence test needs to be scrutinized by Subjects and by colleagues, both those who have had a training in psychology and those who have not so trained. It must be criticized by people with varying training and interests, who should examine it slowly, without time limit, as well as swiftly, within the given time limit. All this should be done *in addition to* the application of techniques such as Item Analysis and various tests for consistency.[1] These techniques are necessary but not sufficient: they do not cut out the need for human collaboration.

And this is the answer to the angry young man's question. The test-constructor with reasonable conscientiousness and humility knows full well and happily that some of his Subjects may be brighter than he is. But he is in the fortunate position of being able to make use of the co-operation and criticism of others, and of working in his own time. If he agrees to develop a new test under pressure, and is willing to say afterwards, 'Yes, that is a weak item. I had to get out the test in a hurry,' he is doing a grave disservice to the mental testing movement. If, on the other hand, he denies that it is a weak item, he is doing an even greater disservice. But if he takes time and advice, he can produce tests that extend people who are considerably more intelligent than he is.

Now to the last comment: 'I suppose these tests are all right for children but some of them are terribly boring for older people.' Children too may find intelligence tests boring, if all the items are of the same form, make use of the same principle and have the same bias. This is one of the reasons why intelligence tests should be 'compounded of many simples, extracted from many objects'. We want to get the best out of our Subjects, be they children or adults. We want them to enjoy the test, for their sake and our own, and they are more likely to do so if they meet variety.

The second reason for varying the form of question and the subject matter is that we are trying to assess *general* intelligence and the wider the scope we offer, the more effectively are we likely to be able to do this. Binet and Wechsler saw this long ago when they constructed their individual scales, with their very varied mediums and subject matter, but the group testers who have followed them have tended to aim for 'purer and purer g' [M], more and more self-consistent tests. This has naturally resulted in series of items which more and more closely resemble one another.[2] This is another growing schism – that between the healthy variety of the individual test and the ingrowing narrowness of the group intelligence test. It is a strange schism to have formed, since almost all psychologists will agree that if a great deal hangs on a particular test score, then it is better to administer an individual test. But they are unaware, apparently, that one of the reasons for the greater satisfactoriness of the individual test is its inclusion of many topics and biases.

When administering intelligence tests we are, or we should be, trying to find out the *strengths* of our Subjects. This is in line with our suggested description of intelligent activity as 'grasping the essentials in a situation and responding appropriately': what is intelligent in one situation may be less so in another, and what is the best move for Johnson may not be the best move – in similar circumstances – for Robinson. It is also a more positive approach than that of trying to ascertain what the Subject *cannot* do. This is the third reason for varying the test material. Some people are happiest and most efficient when thinking visually, others prefer to think verbally, yet others carry out their thought processes, wherever possible, in numerical or other non-verbal symbols. It is true that there are some who do not have very strong predilections towards any of these biases – and they often find it hard to accept these personal idiosyncrasies in others. But such Subjects will do themselves equal justice in a mixed test

The test questions, then, should be varied in form, in bias and in subject matter. The items should be arranged in ascending order of difficulty, as described in Chapter 9, and as is customary group testing procedure. But, in the writer's view, the Subjects should be instructed to take the questions in any order they like. 'Take the questions that appeal to you, first,' they should be told, 'and go back to the others at the end if you have time.' In this way, the Subject with a marked preference (or fear, or dislike) for one or other particular bias can choose as he likes. This is good for his morale and good for showing us what we should want to know – wherein and how far he is gifted.

Most testers will be all too familiar with the anguished cry, 'Oh, but I can't do maths.' often uttered in a situation not very relevant to mathematics. For instance, one of the preliminary examples in a 'mixed' test of high grade intelligence runs as follows.

Working from the left, multiply the third whole number by the fourth decimal:

0·6	3	9	0·7	0·1	0·8	2	4	0·5

This test has been used for the most part with sixth-formers, university candidates and students. It is therefore not surprising that practically all Subjects realize that they are requested to multiply 2 by 0·8. What is surprising, however, is the number of such Subjects who panic when faced with this task and who explain, trembling, that they 'haven't done any maths for ages'. It transpires during the preliminary examples session that, despite their rusty 'mathematics', they are perfectly capable of multiplying 8 by 2 and, after this, of inserting the decimal point, usually in the right place. In fact their initial response is an orectic, rather than a cognitive, one and it is also an unconscious plea not to be subjected to items with a numerical bias.

We shall *learn* that such Subjects 'can't do maths' if they systematically (and without any feeling of guilt) omit all the items containing numbers; but we shall also learn perhaps that they *can* cope very well with words and moderately well with diagrams, if they are not forced to take the questions in the order given. The same argument goes for the (rather less frequent) Subject who, though 'numerate' is not very 'literate'. He experiences an almost equal panic when confronted with verbal items – and if he feels panic-stricken, he is unlikely to behave as intelligently as, in happier circumstances, he could and would. There is some experimental evidence that the very fact of allowing Subjects a fair measure of choice, in itself enables them to do better in mental tests.[3]

Having made this point, it should perhaps be added that when offered the opportunity of taking the questions in any order, many Subjects still do take them in the order presented – with an occasional omission. These Subjects probably do not have very strong positive or negative biases. They enjoy, however, the permissive atmosphere generated by this instruction; and their fellow-Subjects who do have strong feelings about the form of the items will feel happier and will be more likely to show, by means of the test, wherein their gifts lie.

The tester should, then, assemble a variety of items; he should arrange them cyclically (e.g. diagrammatic, verbal, numerical, diagrammatic, verbal, numerical), not in clumps, if the test is to contain equal numbers of the three biases; the questions should be arranged in order of difficulty from the easiest at the beginning to the hardest at the end. This difficulty gradient must be experimentally determined, and applied *within* each type of item. The test items should intercorrelate positively with one another and with the total test score, though these intercorrelations need not be as high as a test-retest correlation needs to be. They will of course be far lower than will the inter-item correlations in a homogeneous test.

The Need for Variety among Intelligence Test Items

It may be recalled that the wail of the 'non-mathematician' above arose in the course of preliminary examples to the test. The importance of conducting such examples immediately before group tests can scarcely be overstated. They should be of the same level of difficulty as the early questions in the test proper. Two illustrations should be given of each type of problem, the first being already completed for the Subject, the second to be filled in by him. Unlimited time should be allowed for these examples, for every Subject should get the examples right before he embarks on the test. Thus he will have made acquaintance with every type of item even if he elects to omit certain types in the test itself. If the Subject makes any errors in the preliminary examples, the tester should encourage him first to read the question aloud and then to think through the problem and try to reach the correct solution. If the tester simply tells the Subject the right answer, even with an explanation, this is of far less use to the Subject in the test proper and is also less good for his self-esteem.[4]

This eliciting of the correct solution is quite a skilled task. It helps to establish rapport between the tester and the tested – a refinement which is often neglected in manuals for group tests. Many text books of psychology go so far as to imply that whilst individual testing is a skilled job, for which the tester must be trained, group testing can be done by virtually anybody who can read the instructions and use a stop-watch. This is an odd way to look at group testing: rapport is just as vital here for satisfactory test results as it is in individual testing and it is in many ways more difficult to establish. Certainly the technique of enlisting interested co-operation from a whole group of people is very different from that of enlisting it from one captive individual.

Apart from encouraging the Subjects to feel that the tester is 'on their side', what are the advantages of administering preliminary examples, as described above? First, they help to disperse the tension or 'examinitis' which many people experience when they find themselves in a test situation and which some few suffer to a crippling degree. Such Subjects feel nervous even when the test is being given for research purposes and as far as they themselves are concerned nothing hangs on the test results. It is still worse for them, of course, if their future is to be part-determined by their test performance. An understanding tester will open the session with a friendly talk and will speak reassuringly, but this will have far less effect than running preliminary examples which demand active participation from the Subject.

When the Subject sees for himself that these are the sorts of question he will be faced with in the test itself, some of his fears vanish. He is not hurried; he has the chance to make and correct his 'nervous' mistakes; he sees others needing help and receiving it. The test is not begun until he has done all the examples and done them correctly – and he *knows* that he has got them right. Some of the more obvious signs of stress are actually seen to decrease during the preliminary examples: hands cease to tremble, sweat ceases to pour, angry disputation changes to humorous backchat.

Secondly, the preliminary examples give the Subject the opportunity of learning what conventions are used in this particular test. As indicated earlier, test constructors attempt to be cogent and objective in their devising of questions, but they do not always succeed. Even those who take time and trouble and submit their early drafts of tests to Subjects and to colleagues for criticism, inevitably incorporate something of their own personality into the test. And the particular conventions they use – which may not seem like conventions to them – will not necessarily be those of their Subjects. The latter need to learn just what is meant by some of the key terms: they may dislike the meaning they learn but during the examples they have the chance to discuss it and they now know how to interpret the questions if they are to do well in the test.

This leads us to the third advantage of preliminary examples, namely, that they imbue the Subject with a sense of having been treated fairly and with respect. If members of the group feel – as they undoubtedly do after having taken certain tests – 'Well, if *that's* what they meant, why didn't they say so?' or 'But that's so trivial, I rejected the idea at once,' this is going to do little good to their image of psychometrics and the test is unlikely to tell the tester 'how good' the Subject could potentially be. It will tell him only how poor, potentially, the Subject could be. If preliminary examples are correctly completed by every member of the group before the test proper, the likelihood of this indignant attitude will be greatly lessened.

Fourthly, examples help to deal with the myth of the 'slow but sure' – who are, indeed, not wholly mythical. There is a small minority of people who are slow starters, sometimes for reasons of temperament, but who go well and reasonably fast, intellectually, once they have grasped the relevant principle. These should not be confused with those who are slow and also inaccurate. For both groups the examples are very necessary but the former group will benefit far more than the latter. The former group consists partly of people who feel impelled to consider every incorrect solution before they allow themselves to contemplate the correct one. This they then accept. If these Subjects settle down to take a test without preliminary examples as described, they are liable to tackle very few questions. They will probably get most of these right but they will still have a far lower score than that of which they are capable.

Fifthly, and finally, we come to the question of differential test-sophistication among Subjects. It is possible that some members of the group being tested have had more experience of psychological tests than others. For some, this may be their first intelligence test; for others, it may be their second or third; yet others may have had a considerable measure of practice plus, perhaps, some coaching. In these circumstances – and they are frequently met, nowadays – it is particularly important to run preliminary examples as outlined above. They will not completely redress the balance but they will go a long way towards levelling up the inexperienced with the practised taker of tests. The former will probably take longer over the examples than will the latter; he will gain far more from them; and he will need to do so.

Practice and coaching for all, over a period of some weeks, is not always feasible (even were it desirable). But concentrated practice-cum-knowledge-of-results, over a period of some minutes immediately preceding the test proper, is a practical proposition which should never be neglected.

9 Speed and Accuracy

With too much quickness ever to be taught;
With too much thinking to have common thought — ALEXANDER POPE

*Ungenerous time limit – Gradient of difficulty –
Inseparability of speed and accuracy*

This chapter on the question of speed and power in intelligence testing falls into two parts. In the first part, the traditional attitude towards speed and power in cognitive tests is outlined. In the second part, some comments on this attitude are offered and a few suggestions are made as to how the problem might be tackled in practice. That it is something of a problem is clear from the priority often given to the objection that 'these are simply tests of speed', usually followed by the assertion that 'you have to be quick and slick to do well on them'. This criticism comes in the main from the less informed sectors of the population but it is stated and restated with sound and fury. This is not to suggest that it signifies nothing. In the above form, however, it is an overstatement.

The argument runs as follows. Group tests are timed and the time limit allowed is, designedly, ungenerous. Therefore, most members of the tested group fail to reach the end. Therefore the people who do best will be those who work fastest. Therefore the test is one of speed.

Whilst it is true that the time limit is deliberately ungenerous in most group tests of intelligence, yet for a number of reasons the conclusions do not follow. The implication is that the vast majority of the Subjects get right the vast majority of the questions they attempt and hence that their score is a function of their speed. But if the relation between test level and group level is correctly gauged, it will not be the case that most of the Subjects get right most of the questions attempted. We shall return to this point later.

The reasons for imposing a time limit in group testing, and for allowing only a short time relative to the length of the test, are administrative. It is not practicable to allow unlimited time, as is usual in most individual tests of intelligence, for group members differ enormously in their preferred rate of working. On the same test, the time taken by Subjects working in their own time can easily range from twenty minutes to an hour or more.[1] Thus the tester cannot ask his Subjects – as he would like to do – to work at their own speed and let him know when they have finished. The test would in effect be *a different test* for the Subject who finished in twenty minutes and the one who took an hour. Their results would not be comparable, and comparability is the main purpose of testing: an objective means of differentiating is required.

These great individual differences in speed of work supply the reason for the shortness of the time allowed in group tests. In order for the results to be comparable, everyone in the group needs to have been working throughout. It is of no use to the tester if some finish with, say, ten seconds and some finish with ten minutes, to spare. To ensure, then, that all group members use the whole of the testing time, a time limit is set which is so short that none but the very fastest reach the end in the time allowed. It is desirable, incidentally, to tell the Subjects at the end of the session that they should not worry if they have not finished and that very few people do reach the end of the test. Since some Subjects feel frustrated at being stopped, and others feel a sense of failure at not reaching the end, it is desirable also to go into the matter with them in the discussion – which should, in the writer's opinion, always take place after testing for those who are interested.

If a case has now been made for the imposition of an ungenerous time limit in group testing, what precautions are taken to ensure that the test assesses 'much thinking' as well as 'much quickness'? The gradient of difficulty, described below, is one method which is nearly always used. This gradient means that the questions are arranged in order of difficulty, the easiest items being presented at the beginning, the harder ones later and the most difficult problems right at the end of the test.

The relative levels of difficulty are established experimentally – not determined from the depths of an armchair – during the development of the test. In order to do this, the items are offered in randomized order and preferably in unlimited time, to several hundreds of Subjects of the type for whom the test is intended. Thus every problem will have been tackled by a (random) majority of the Subjects. This is important because otherwise certain of the questions might be attempted by a minority of Subjects only – and this minority might well be unrepresentatively bright. Having ensured then that virtually every member of the group has tried every question, it is meaningful to calculate the percentage of correct answers given to each problem. From this Table of percentages the best order of the questions can be worked out.

At this stage, an item analysis can be made too of the *incorrect* responses, in order to gain more information about the questions and to eliminate those that are statistically unsatisfactory [N]. But this is not strictly relevant to the problem of speed and power.

The choice of question order is fairly straightforward in a test all of whose items are identical in form. If, however, the test contains items using different principles (e.g. series, analogies, features in common, sames) and/or different biases (e.g. numerical, pictorial, verbal, diagrammatic), then the gradient of difficulty should be arranged within each item-type. For instance, the second numerical series item should be harder than the first numerical series item and easier than the third. We are not directly concerned with the level of difficulty of the series items *vis-à-vis* the verbal analogies or the pictorial sames. In fact, a smooth overall difficulty gradient in a 'mixed' test is not feasible for all Subjects: the correct order for a 'verbal Subject' would be different from the correct order for a 'visual Subject'. Within the various types of question, however, the correct order will be pretty constant among Subjects. It is unlikely that adjacent items will come out wildly unevenly if the test as a whole is reasonably homogeneous with regard to level of difficulty.

The rationale for having a gradient of difficulty is twofold. First, it is hoped to reduce the importance of the speed factor in group tests. The argument is that a Subject who is quick, slick and thoughtless will romp through the test attempting all, or nearly all, of the questions, and maintaining his swiftness throughout. He will thus fail on a good many of the harder problems (those he will meet in the latter part of the test) – since, *ex hypothesi*, although fast he is not very intelligent – and his score will be unimpressive. On the other hand, the slow but sure Subject will attempt far fewer questions, these will be relatively easy since they come near the beginning; and he will of course get right a very high proportion of them, achieving a reasonably good score.

The Subject who is both slow and inaccurate will do worst; and the lucky chap who combines high speed with high accuracy will do best. This seems satisfactory test-wise and it tallies with most people's view of intelligent activity outside the psychological laboratory.

The second reason for building a difficulty gradient into the test is that this enables the early questions to constitute training for the harder questions; and the harder questions constitute training for the hardest ones. This continues the process which was begun in the preliminary examples, if these have been competently administered. Like the examples, the gradient familiarizes the Subject with the particular propensities of the test-constructor and it also oils the Subject's psychological wheels. If one picks up a new intelligence test and goes straight to the last page, one may well find a number of apparently insoluble problems on it. The most frequent reaction to this is a burst of righteous anger. If, however, one turns back to the earlier questions one will usually find (if the test be sound) that working through them makes clear what is required in the later questions. This may be regarded by the opponent of tests as a kind of unworthy indoctrination. It is unlikely to be so regarded by the potential Subject and – unworthy or not – it will not generalize and spread, dangerously, into other fields.

So far a case has been made that group intelligence tests do not merely test speed; that speed does play some part, however, in addition to careful, accurate thinking; and that this is as it should be, since if two people both solve a difficult problem, the first solving it faster than the second, the former would generally be said to be the more able or intelligent of the two. This is not only a matter of general agreement, however. A number of experiments have been carried out on intelligence tests, in which the Subjects have been instructed to take a test first with a time limit and then in unlimited time.[1] Other experiments have been done using parallel tests, again with and without time limit. Score on unlimited time has been compared with score on limited time, insofar as this is feasible. Score gained in unlimited time has been correlated too with length of time actually taken by each Subject for choice. The results have usually shown a low but significant negative correlation, i.e. a tendency for the people who work faster for choice to gain a higher score on unlimited time and for people who work more slowly for choice to gain a lower score on unlimited time. This suggests that the assumption of speed going on the whole with accuracy, and not against it, may have some justification. It should be remembered, however, that the correlation is generally low and, moreover, that it is due largely to a 'tail' of Subjects – a small minority who are exceptionally slow and exceptionally inaccurate.

The traditional attitude towards speed and power in cognitive tests has now been sympathetically outlined. I believe that this attitude is largely justified. But I would join issue with those psychometrists who go further, who believe that speed/power is a dichotomy (similar to those deplored in Chapter 1); that speed and power are two 'factors' to be taken into account when considering the 'structure of the mind' (a somewhat misleading phrase, often used by factor-analytically-minded psychologists);[2] and that it is possible to devise tests of power and tests of speed, separately.[3]

In the writer's view such a dichotomy is invalid. The same test can be largely a test of speed for one group – whose members find the test easy, and largely a test of power (or accuracy, or level) for another group – for whom the test is difficult. It can be transformed from a speed test to a power test, and conversely, by means of changing the instructions. Identical questions, as has been shown in Chapter 6, can become harder (and therefore more 'powerful') or easier (and therefore more a matter of speed) according to the context in which the questions appear. If upward and downward adaptation to level of difficulty is a reality, then it is clear that the static notion of a 'speed test' or a 'power test' is inapplicable.[4]

The extent to which a test assesses speed or power depends on the relationship between the level of the test and the level of the group taking the test. If the test is too easy (or the group 'too intelligent') the Subjects' score will be largely a measure of their speed, since they will get right a very high proportion of what they attempt. If the test is a great deal too difficult for the Subjects, then their responses will approach random answering and no meaningful differentiation among them will be achieved.

An example of the latter phenomenon occurred in some experiments which the writer and her colleagues were conducting some years ago in a secondary modern boys' school. These (fourteen-year-old) boys took several cognitive tests including AH5, a test of high-grade intelligence designed for the top ten to fifteen per cent of the population. One of the aims of including this test was to ascertain just *how* unsuitable it was for adolescents whose 'top people' had already been creamed off. The results were interesting in that the vast majority of these boys did reach the end of the test – and did gain very low scores, many of them around chance. They did not realize how difficult the test items were; they worked much faster than brighter Subjects of the same age; and they obtained far lower scores.

It is worth emphasizing that a pure speed test should entirely neglect accuracy. Thus a test consisting of groups of digits, for instance, in which the Subject is asked to cross out every 2 and every 9 is *not* a pure test of speed (not even of a highly specialized kind of speed), if the score is the total number of 2s and 9s that are cancelled in the time. Most so-called tests of speed set the Subject a task and ask him to do it as quickly as possible. If notice is taken of his errors or his omissions, however, this is not a pure test of speed. In the Word-in-context test (see Chapter 5) the number of sets attempted is a measure of speed, since this is recorded *regardless of the correctness of the answers given*. There are probably very few cognitive situations, however, in which the assessment of speed alone and uncontaminated is a useful measure.

Speed and accuracy, and the relations between them, depend partly on the intellect of the Subject and partly on his temperament. His reaction to the test is the outcome of his total personality, and the interaction of this with the tester and the instructions. There are few grounds for believing that this interaction will be constant for the same Subject when presented with different tests, administered by different testers. Indeed there is quite a lot of evidence to suggest that it will vary, and that it will vary more for some Subjects than for others.

10   The Use of Questionnaires in Orectic Studies

Not men but measures – BURKE

Multiple-choice questionnaires in orectic studies – Unwelcome
response styles – The E.P.I. Test – The Study of Values

To judge from the plethora of text books on psychological testing, men – like tests – are conveniently divisible into cognitive
elements and non-cognitive elements. Many psychometrists, such
as Guilford, seem to believe that we get a good deal more out of
our tests than we put in: that we can actually learn something of
the nature of men by means of feeding them tests and analysing
the test results.[1] Since these results depend on the particular
tests and Subjects used, and the conclusions drawn depend on the
particular technique of analysis selected, this seems an ingenuous-
ly optimistic outlook. The choice of tests, of Subjects and of
factor-analytical method is often very arbitrary, and the interpretation of results equally so. Hence the conflict of theories
found over the years, even among authorities in the field.

In my opinion, it is 'not men but measures' about which
information is being stockpiled. We should be chary of translat-
ing our findings about measures into conclusions about men –
though this is not to say that the measures are valueless. I am
strongly in favour of developing new and better measures. By
this is meant, cognitive tests which are cogent, consistent, and
validated against non-test criteria; orectic tests which do not
insult the intelligence, perceptiveness and sense of humour of the
Subjects taking them and which also are validated against non-
test criteria. It is with the latter tests that this chapter and the subsequent one are concerned.

Group tests of temperament, character and interests will be
discussed. These are usually referred to by psychologists as 'personality tests', but this nomenclature will be avoided for the
reasons given in Chapter 6. First, a general description will be

given of those tests which are designated usually as questionnaires or 'personality inventories'. We are not concerned here with individual, projective tests such as the Rorschach[2] and the Thematic Apperception Test,[3] but only with group tests. Secondly two well-known and widely used tests, the E.P.I.[4] and the Study of Values,[5] will be outlined and discussed. In the next chapter, a description will be given of a more recent (open-ended) test being developed by the writer and her colleagues, which attempts to overcome some of the difficulties inherent in a multiple-choice type orectic test.

The typical multiple-choice questionnaire is a paper and pencil test which asks the Subject questions about himself and his relations with other individuals and groups. The test is usually untimed but the Subjects are instructed not to spend too long on any one item. The questions often assume a high degree of self-knowledge, and also of intimacy between the Subject and the tester. In fact the tests occasionally ask questions which, in England at least, one's nearest and dearest would hesitate to ask – and even they would not be surprised to receive in reply a facetious or embarrassed half-truth.

The multiple-choice items, however, offer little scope for subtle half-truths. They either give a robust, no-nonsense choice of 'Yes/No', on issues which may be quite complex (as, for instance, the Cornell Index,[6] of which a typical question is 'Are you often misunderstood? – Yes/No'). Or the items may be in the form of questions to which the Subject is asked to reply on, say, a five-point scale. For example, 'Do you often feel just miserable? – Almost always/Frequently/Occasionally/Rarely/Almost never'. This is from the M.M.P.I. test.[7] Another variant of the five-point scale type is in the form of statements against which the Subject records his degree of agreement. An illustration (again from the M.M.P.I.): 'Laws are so often made for the benefit of small selfish groups that a man cannot respect the law – Strongly agree/Agree/Undecided/Disagree/Strongly disagree'.

This form is open to the objection that Subjects who feel they know their own mind may dislike the wording of the middle way, 'Undecided'. Indeed it is difficult to frame the wording of the middle way to everybody's satisfaction. The last example has, too, the disadvantage of being double-barrelled: the Subject may want to indicate, for instance, that he has little respect for the law – but for some reason other than that given; or he may agree that laws are often made for the benefit of small selfish groups, and yet still respect the law.

The five-point scale items are, however, an improvement on the simple Yes/No form, partly because they are somewhat less frustrating to the Subject and partly because they yield more information – not only five points as opposed to two, but also as to whether the Subject is more inclined to extremes or to the middle way, at least in his responses. This form, moreover, is less liable to arouse 'acquiescence response style', that is, the tendency on the part of Subjects to agree rather than disagree with a suggestion, other things being equal.

Psychometrists have gone to considerable trouble, first to discover experimentally the various 'response styles' and then to compensate for them in their tests.[8] Another of these is 'social desirability response style' – a tiresome characteristic, from the point of view of the tester, to which Subjects taking questionnaires have been found to be notoriously prone. This refers to the Subject's tendency to make himself out to be a more acceptable and likeable person than he is or, at least, to make himself appear as he thinks (unconsciously perhaps) the tester would like him to be. This tendency is, of course, by no means confined to orectic test Subjects. The individual who does not make himself out to be a little kinder, a little cleverer and a little more honest (inside or outside the test situation) than he is in practice most of the time, is rare indeed. In fact, people who do not make this attempt are probably not quite normal, statistically speaking – and 'normality' has little or no meaning, other than statistically.

The question of honesty is particularly important when considering personality inventories. Psychometrists have usually taken one of two approaches to this problem.

Firstly, they say that the honesty and self-knowledge of the Subject are quite irrelevant. It does not matter whether he answers, or even knows, the truth about himself. They claim to be working purely operationally. Thus what they are concerned with is the establishing of a relationship between a certain pattern of test scores and the prescribed criterion. If this relationship is statistically significant, they say, this is all that is needed. The test has justified itself; it is validated; it does not matter what you *call* it. This stance is sometimes a shade unconvincing, in view of the particular questions comprising most personality inventories. It is defensible, however, as long as the criterion is not altered or repudiated in mid-stream and the test is not given the name of some human attribute, or collection of attributes, which already have a generally accepted, non-test connotation. (An example of this sort of behaviour is given on page 17.)

The second approach consists of building into the test various measures intended to counteract the reprehensible response style of the Subject. In particular, some psychometrists insert 'lie-detectors', i.e. certain items intended to enable the tester to spot the Subject who is more dishonest than most. In my view, these so-called lie-detectors have two snags: (*i*) They constitute short tests of *intelligence* rather than honesty. Indeed, the intelligent Subject is capable of answering these items 'honestly' and the non-lie-detector items 'dishonestly'. (*ii*) Their inclusion in the test plays havoc with the statement generally included in the instructions to orectic tests, that 'there are no right or wrong answers'. These points may become clearer, if a concrete example is taken.

Let us first, then, consider the E.P.I.[9] This test consists of two parallel forms, A and B, both of which set out to measure Extraversion and Neuroticism. The authors claim that these two factors are unrelated to each other. They write:

While not wishing to deny the existence and importance of factors additional to E and N, we believe that these two factors contribute more to a description of personality than any other set of two factors outside the cognitive field.

(Note, in passing, the odd meaning of 'personality' unashamedly adopted here.) This test has been chosen because it illustrates most of the points raised above, about personality inventories. It consists of fifty-seven questions, all in Yes/No form; as will be seen, the test is particularly instructive on the matter of acquiescence response style; many of the questions are of a highly intimate nature; insofar as any validation data are offered, these are concerned with the relationship between E and N scores and certain criterion groups (whose results by no means always go in the predicted direction); and the tests contain 'a Lie Scale', designed to recognize those Subjects showing 'desirability response set'.

Two illustrations, one drawn from Form A and the other from Form B, will serve to exemplify the type of question used. (a) 'Are you troubled with feelings of inferiority? – Yes/No'. (b) 'Do you worry too long after an embarrassing experience? – Yes/No'. These questions suffer from the defect of crudity in the sense that it is abundantly clear, even to an unsophisticated Subject, how he should respond if he wishes to appear 'stable' and how he should respond if he wishes to appear neurotic. There is, moreover, a certain absurdity in asking anyone if he worries *too* long after a certain experience.

On the matter of acquiescence response style there is a further crudity here, namely, the fact that the 'neurotic' (or should one say neuroticistic?) response to all the N items is in fact 'Yes' (as is clear in the two examples given above). There are two objections to this: first, that, as in most psychological tests, it is desirable to ring the changes on the significant responses, whether the choice be from two or more, in order to avoid the Subject's just encircling all the responses in the same column, be it the Yeses or the Noes. Secondly, whilst there may be an association between acquiescence response style (or suggestibility) and neuroticism (or neurosis) these two are certainly not identical. And it would be helpful in a test of this kind, to be able to distinguish between them. Furthermore, many Subjects feel angrily that it is foolish to offer this type of question in a Yes/No form. Similar objections apply to the Extraversion items, for example, 'Generally, do you prefer reading to meeting people? – Yes/No'. It is not only the intellectual who mutters in his beard, 'Depends on the book – depends on the people'.

The examples quoted illustrate not only the inadequacy of the Yes/No method but also the high degree of intimacy assumed by the tester: his evident willingness to plunge feet first into topics which many Subjects will regard as their own private business. The two areas about which people tend to feel most touchy are their feelings and their health, physical and mental. Both are swiftly tackled here: e.g. 'Do you get attacks of shaking or trembling?' 'Do you suffer from nerves?' and 'Do you worry about your health?' . . .

These criticisms would carry little weight, however, if the validation of the test were satisfactory. If – despite these 'face-validity' objections – convincing evidence were given that the test does effect discrimination, as predicted, between various criterion groups, one might be inclined to say that 'it works' and with this short phrase bulldoze the idea that the Subject's attitude is important and that the Yes/No technique is inappropriate. But examination of the short section in the E.P.I. Test Manual on validation,[10] and of the two Tables on criterion groups,[11] reveals that such validation as is offered is unconvincing.

In the first place, the authors write:

One possible criterion of validity which is in line with procedure in the more exact sciences is that the test should fit in with predictions made from a more general theory. This type of validation exists in profusion in relation to the M.P.I.[12] (Knapp, 1962[13]); in virtue of the close similarity of the E.P.I. scales to those of the M.P.I. it seems reasonable to argue that this proof would also apply to the new scales. Independent proof would, of course, be required in due course, but is not yet available.

It is perfectly true that the E.P.I. closely resembles the M.P.I. In fact it is almost indistinguishable from it. To quote from the Sixth Mental Measurements Yearbook:[14]

Although the E.P.I. and the M.P.I. are differently named, they are the same tests, in respect to principal authorship, theoretical motivation, traits measured and methodological derivation. Indeed some items in the two tests are but rewordings of each other.

But the validation which 'exists in profusion' for the M.P.I. is striking in its quantity rather than its quality and to say that 'independent proof *would*, *of course*, *be* required in due course but is *not yet available*' (my italics) smacks of complacent irresponsibility unless the remaining data given on validation are satisfactory.

The subsequent paragraph in the Validity section of the E.P.I. Manual, however, provides an excellent example of the repudiation of a criterion in mid-stream, mentioned earlier in this chapter (page 18). Eysenck and Eysenck write that they have shown

that when independent judges are asked to nominate extraverted and introverted, or stable and unstable Subjects, and when these nominees are then asked to fill in the E.P.I. . . . there are clear and predictable differences on the scales between the respective *extreme* groups [present writer's italics].

But, they go on to say that

there is some evidence that where there is lack of agreement, it is the judges who are at fault, rather than the inventory answers.

Heads I win, tails you lose.

The third type of 'validation' data offered are in the form of Tables listing the mean scores of various Normal and Abnormal groups on the E.P.I. scales. In principle, criterion groups are an excellent method of test validation but some of these figures confirm the doubts about E.P.I. validity already raised by reading the text. For example, the mean Extraversion scores of apprentices and G.P.O. telephonists (normal group) are, respectively, 29·288 and 24·783, whilst those of depressives and schizophrenics are, respectively, 23·317 and 21·865. Again, on the Neuroticism score, the mean of the (normal) army Subjects, 20·812, is virtually the same as the mean of the schizophrenics, 20·843. (Note, incidentally, the high level of 'accuracy' with which the mean scores are given: the presentation of means, correct to three places of decimal – derived from test items the significance of which is doubtful.)

Validation, then, is questionable. Consistency – always a difficult matter in orectic tests – is not even mentioned. Let us consider the Lie Scale which, it is claimed, enables the tester to spot Subjects showing 'desirability response set'. The reader is

told that the Lie Scale 'may be used to eliminate' such Subjects –
but he is not told what to do with the eliminated Subjects.
Eysenck comments in another paper that 'where people are
motivated to try and give as good an account of themselves as
possible, questionnaires are almost useless'.[15] This may well be
true of multiple-choice questionnaires but if so it would reduce
their application exclusively to pure research – and even then
certain Subjects would merit 'elimination'. Yet the E.P.I. authors
state with respect to individual testing that 'for purposes of
diagnosis and treatment, the E.P.I. should be administered
routinely'. They recommend it, in addition, for psychiatric and
medical research work in the industrial field.

Let us now inspect some of the items inserted as 'lie-detectors'.
'Have you ever been late for an appointment or work? – Yes/No.'
'Do you sometimes get cross? – Yes/No.' The instructions printed
on the first page of the test end with the sentence: 'There are no right
or wrong answers, and this isn't a test of intelligence or ability,
but simply a measure of the way you behave.' In my view, there *is*
a right answer to both these items, namely 'Yes'. If there were
not a 'right answer' they could scarcely be lie-detecting items. Furthermore, to give the 'wrong' answer in most of such cases would
indicate lack of intelligence rather than lack of honesty.

The E.P.I. was chosen for detailed discussion because it is a
British test; its near-identical predecessor has been extensively
used (117 references in the Sixth Mental Measurement Yearbook); it is in many ways typical of multiple-choice personality
inventories; it exemplifies well all the points raised for discussion.
It consists of apparently simple, highly intimate questions to be
answered either Yes or No, its validation is sparse and unconvincing and its Lie Scale gives the lie to its own Instructions.

Let us now examine a very different type of questionnaire, the
Study of Values.[5,16] This again is a multiple-choice, forced-
choice, primarily orectic test but it is concerned with personal
interests. Its authors call the test a 'Values' study because it is
derived from Spranger's *Types of Men*,[17] which postulated the
existence of six 'ideal types' of men having major values of the six
types, comprising the Study of Values Test. Nearly all of the

enquiries making use of the test, however, employ it as a test of intrinsic interests. It is chosen here because it ranks high both in applied work and as a research instrument – it has 280 references in the Sixth Mental Measurements Yearbook – and it differs in many ways from the E.P.I. It is in two parts, Part I being in the form of statements or questions, each followed by '(a) Yes. (b) No.'

All the evidence that has been impartially accumulated goes to show that the universe has evolved to its present state in accordance with mechanistic principles, so that there is no need to assume a first cause, cosmic purpose, or God behind it. (a) Yes. (b) No.

Since the class or social status to which a man belongs depends mainly on his push and ability, it is just that a small proportion of the population should be very rich. (a) Yes. (b) No.

In this test, however, the Subject is not forced to put all his psychological eggs into one positive or negative basket. He is asked, if he agrees with alternative (a) and disagrees with (b), to respond thus, (a) 3, (b) 0. But if he has only a slight preference for (a) over (b), he is to respond, (a) 2, (b) 1. Similarly for definite or slight (b) preferences. Thus Part I of this test does not over-simplify to the same extent as does plain Yes/No answering though, as is clear from the two illustrations given, our old enemy, the double-barrelled question, still rears its head. This difficulty is particularly important with the sixth-former and student type of Subject for whom this test is primarily intended.

Part II consists of fifteen questions, each followed by four different courses. For instance:

If you should marry (or are married) do you prefer a wife who (a) can achieve social prestige, commanding admiration from others, (b) likes to stay at home and keep house, (c) is fundamentally spiritual in her attitude to life, (d) is gifted along artistic lines.

For women Subjects, this question is worded as follows:

If you should marry (or are married) do you prefer a husband who: (a) is successful in his profession, commanding admiration from others, (b) is domestic in his tastes, (c) is fundamentally spiritual in his attitude to life, (d) is gifted along artistic lines.

The instructions to the Subject for Part II are to arrange the answers in order of personal preference from first to fourth by writing on the answer sheet:

1 beside the letter corresponding to the answer that appeals to you most,

2 beside the letter corresponding to the answer which is next most important to you,

3 beside the letter corresponding to the next, and

4 beside the letter corresponding to the answer that least represents your interest or preference.

The Subject is told that he must make his selection from the alternatives presented; that he should guess when his preferences are not distinct; and that if he 'finds it really impossible to guess' his preferences, he may omit the question.

Thus the test is less rigid and authoritarian than the E.P.I. but the Subject is still not allowed to say that all the courses suggested to him appeal equally – or that, say, two of them do – nor that he cordially dislikes them all. Each of these three very different attitudes would come out as omissions in the case of a serious-minded Subject and would be scored in the same way, namely, *equally* weighted for each of the alternatives. He is not, of course, allowed to offer any suggestions of his own. This regimentation is irritating to some Subjects and it appears less than satisfactory to the present writer; certain potentially useful data are being ignored.

It is the conscientious, co-operative Subjects who make heavy weather of this sort of situation. The light-hearted and flippant, or thoughtless, either do not notice or take the line that if this game gives pleasure to the tester, they are not going to spoil his fun. They obediently answer the sometimes unanswerable questions in the predetermined way, at a speed which delights their tester. But the serious-minded either appear obstructive, asserting that they cannot do the task set; or they respond, consciously or unconsciously, in the way which seems to them most socially desirable.

The *Study of Values* is intended to assess six interests or values, namely, 'Theoretical, Economic, Aesthetic, Social, Political and

Religious'. Most of these have roughly the meaning that is customarily assigned to them but there is a note at the end of the test stating that 'the term "economic" indicates "having an eye to the main chance" – "being predominantly concerned with material values"; whilst the term "political" denotes in general "power seeking" – "interested in managing people."' This strikes me as yet another example of psychologists' using ordinary, non-technical words to connote meanings overlapping with – but not identical with – the meanings usually assigned to them, and probably assigned by the Subjects who take the test. This seems to be a pity, especially when the test aims to assess interests or 'values'.

Even if this stretched (and shrunk) meaning of 'political' be accepted, however, some of the items seem to be a far cry from the interest nominally measured. Consider, for instance, the following question.

Which of the following would you prefer to do during part of your next summer vacation (if your abilities and other conditions would permit): (a) write and publish an original biological essay or article, (b) stay in some secluded part of the country where you can appreciate fine scenery, (c) go to a local tennis or other athletic tournament, (d) get experience in some new line of business.

In this item, a Subject who prefers (c) is marked up on 'political' – and this is not the only item in which a preference for sport is scored as a political interest. To the present writer it seems that such answers are not evidence of political interest either in the usual sense (of current affairs, elections, political parties) or in the special sense chosen in the *Study of Values*. Sport and athletics is a fairly clear interest category and does not, in the writer's opinion, go particularly frequently with political interests, however this phrase is interpreted.

A further objection to such questionnaires is that a high score on one interest automatically ensures a low score on one or more other interests, and conversely. Such tests imply the assumption that there is just so much 'interest-ability' in all of us – an *equal* amount in all of us – and, therefore, if the Subject has many interests his profile will be flattish, i.e. a rather uniform and low level of enthusiasm generally will emerge. A similar flattish profile will be found for the Subject who has *no* interests – and undoubtedly Subjects exist who are not much interested in any of the six for which the *Study of Values* caters. Again, someone markedly lacking in interest x will be found to show up highly on interest y or z, as a direct result of the ipsative scoring system and the forced-choice technique. Yet the existence of people whose interests are both wide and deep, and of others whose interests are both narrow and shallow, cannot be denied.

Finally, the multiple-choice method by its very nature, does not allow the Subject to show any enterprise or individuality in his interests. No scope is offered for someone with unusual interests, or even with strong contra-suggestibility, to portray himself, whether he will or no. Tests of this kind which claim to be assessing an important facet of personality are 'closed-ended' to the highest degree. This is surely less permissible in orectic tests than in cognitive tests, where there is intended to be one, and only one, right answer.

This chapter has consisted largely of criticism. The next chapter is more constructive: in it a test is described which aims to assess the temperament traits and the interests mentioned above – plus some others – but which is not open to the same objections.

11 The Brook Reaction Test

You would play upon me; you would seem to know my stops; you would pluck out the heart of my mystery; you would sound me from my lowest note to the top of my compass—SHAKESPEARE

The Brook Reaction Test – Testing of interests – System of scoring – Assessment of temperament – Validity and consistency

This chapter concerns a test which is still being standardized and which looks suspiciously like developing into a General Purposes test. It was originally designed as a test of personal interests, in an attempt to overcome the difficulties described in Chapter 10. It was, therefore, to be open-ended – in order to avoid the problems arising from multiple-choice, forced-choice and double-barrelled questions – yet objectively scorable, and administrable in group-test form. It was not to probe brashly into the innermost hopes and doubts of the Subjects nor to allow of the hazards of un-welcome response styles or of faking. It was to cater for widely varying amounts of 'interestability' within Subjects and to enable the original or eccentric to give full rein to their individualism. It was of course essential that the test should correlate highly with other measures of interests.

The test is called the Brook Reaction Test of Interests and it looks as though it does indeed assess personal interests and is not open to the objections of the questionnaire type of test.[1] But somewhat to the surprise of the Brook's devisers, it looks too as though the test has direct clinical application – not merely by virtue of the assessment of personal interests, but also in its recognition of the disturbed and the excessively introverted. Its technique and scoring system as a measure of twenty-two interests is discussed first; then the evidence for its value as a diagnostic instrument for spotting the neurotic, psychotic or otherwise disturbed, is outlined [P]; and, finally, some evidence is given of the Brook's validity and consistency.

The Brook Reaction test is a form of word-association test.[2] It derives its name from the late David Brook, who was partly responsible for selecting the original stimulus words and for testing Subjects when the test was in its earliest form.[3] It is generally used as a group paper-and-pencil test, but like any other group test it can be given individually, when this is thought desirable. The Instructions have been tape-recorded and they are played to the group when all Subjects are comfortably seated and spaced at tables or desks and have in front of them a Brook Response Sheet and a pencil. The recorded Instructions are as follows:

This test is a reaction test. It's very simple and there are no right or wrong answers. I am going to say a word and I want you to write down the first word that comes to mind after that, and then what the word you have written reminds you of, and so on.

For instance, if I said HOT, you might put 'cold ice skating'; or you might go on to 'sun rise East'; or something quite different. To the word DINNER, you might reply 'table wood tree': or perhaps 'eat drink beer'; or again you might put something quite different. Now, I'll give you an example to do, to make sure you get the idea, before we start the test proper. Will you put down your answers now to the word WINDOW.

Start the stop-watch for twelve seconds. During this period, (*a*) make sure that everyone has begun writing, (*b*) say, 'Write as many words as possible', (*c*) at the end of the twelve seconds: 'Will you stop now.'

Go round to see that all Subjects have written at least two words and have got the idea.

Now, one more example before we start. Will you please now put down your answers to NEWSPAPER. (Twelve seconds.) Right, will you please stop now.

Check as before.

Those were just examples to see that you understood the instructions. (Short pause.) Now please turn over to page 2 and fold your paper back. (Pause twenty seconds.)

Right. There will be two pages of test words. You see that your page is numbered from 1 to 40; this is for the first half of the test. There is one line for each set of answers. Don't write the word I say but try to write at least three words in reply to it. Be sure to put your answers by the right number each time.

We've tried to make every word as clear as possible. But if you're not sure of a particular word, please write down your answer to what you think you heard.

No questions can be answered once the test has begun, so if you have any please ask now. Are there any questions? (Twenty-eight second pause – during which tester stops tape, if necessary. Restart tape after questions, if any, have been dealt with.)

Ready, now: No. 1, CANVAS (Twelve-second pause) No. 2, BANK (Twelve-second pause) No. 3, ...

It will be seen that the stimulus words chosen for the preliminary examples are simple and unambiguous. It is thought that these examples of words with only one meaning help to establish a set towards one-meaning interpretation of the test words – although, as anticipated, the single meaning assumed in the test proper varies from Subject to Subject. The stimulus words used in the test itself (though also simple) are ambiguous: all have at least two meanings and the majority have three or more. The categorization of interests depends on the sense of the stimulus word assumed by the Subject.

Thus, in reply to the stimulus, CANVAS(s), the Subject may write, for instance, 'oils painting Picasso' or 'painting portrait' (*Aesthetic*); 'material clothes' or 'cloth dress shoes' (*Clothing and appearance*); 'circus Harlequin cages' or 'flats stage footlights' (*Entertainment*); 'linoleum floor polish' or 'cover hole drill' (*Practical*); 'sail boat' or 'tent camping countryside stream' (*Outdoor activities*); 'voting parties Labour Conservative' or 'election polling' (*Political*); 'ring boxing lights' (*Sport*).

Thus the interest category into which the response is placed is reasonably objective. Occasionally the response does not imply any of the twenty-two interests, in which case it is categorized as *Unclassifiable*. Examples of Unclassifiable responses to the stimulus-word CANVAS would be 'hard cold shiny' or 'light match smoke'. All the above illustrations are drawn from the hundreds of responses that have in fact been given in reply to CANVAS(S).

The Subjects are not told the purpose of the test beforehand; they do not suspect it during the course of the test; and very few of them realize that all the stimulus words are ambiguous. Most manage to write at least two response-words in the time allowed; many produce three; and responses of four, and even five, words are not unknown. A few Subjects reply with '*Multiple Themes*', that is, they respond to several different meanings of the stimulus word, e.g. SERVICE → 'restaurant tennis church'. The majority, however, confine themselves to one theme per stimulus word – though some people do go off at a tangent to one of their own response-words. Examples of the latter would be: ANGLE → 'acute chronic', BANK → 'notes flute Bach'.

Table I shows the complete list of the twenty-two interest categories, for which the Brook caters. This is a replica of the Rating Sheet which has been used, among other methods, for Brook validation – about which more, later.

Several points should be made about Table I. First, it is perhaps worth pointing out that what may broadly be called 'social' interests have been split into three categories: *D* for *Dances*, parties and social functions generally; *H* for *Humanitarian* – which might perhaps be described briefly as oriented towards the social sciences; and *PE* for *People*, i.e. persons as individuals, including children in their own right. This tripartite division of 'social' responses was suggested to us by early experience with the test. The three proved to be interestingly different and by no means always associated with one another in practice.

In a similar way, we learned to divide what had originally been designated simply as 'scientific' into two separate categories, *Physical Science* (*SN*) and *Biological Science* (*SB*), despite the fact that these two categories have many concepts and many terms in common. As will be seen, however, the scoring system allows for responses to be split, where necessary, between two or more of these categories. Such splitting is often found to be desirable, also, between the *Practical* (*K*) ^{Q} and the *Physical Science* categories. These and several other categories are recog-

Rating on .... by ......,.........................

Please read the instructions carefully and then fill in the appropriate number in each of the 22 spaces.

INSTRUCTIONS

5 = Extremely interested
4 = Very much interested
3 = Some definite interest
2 = Mildly interested
1 = Minimum of interest. Very rarely do anything about it
0 = No interest at all. Never think, talk or do anything along these lines
-1 = Positively anti. Actively object to the topic in question

Interests

A = aesthetic. Interests in the arts, especially music, painting and sculpture.
B = business. Finance, trade, commerce, economics, money-making ....
C = clothing. Personal appearance and dress. Materials (textiles) ....
D = dances, parties and social functions generally ....
E = entertainment. Theatre, films, wireless and television ....
F = food and drink ....
G = agriculture and farming; gardening and horticulture ....
H = humanitarian. Interested in people generally, rather than in individual persons. Social service, welfare organizations, social sciences, human problems ....
I = intellectual interests. Discussing and thinking about abstract ideas: includes historical and theoretical matters.
K = practical. 'Do it Yourself' interest; keenness on crafts, gadgets, machines; helping at home ....
LT = literary. Books and writers; prose and poetry ....
LW = law. Legal matters and things connected with the law generally ....
M = military, including all the Armed Forces ....
O = outdoor activities. Camping, boating, fishing, walking, mountaineering. Love of the countryside
PE = people. Interested in people as individuals; in children; in human personality ....
PL = political. Current affairs, elections, political parties, unions ....
R = religion. Church-going, the bible; and/or religion plays an important part in life ....
S B = biological sciences: medical, botanical, zoological interests. Natural history ....
S N = physical sciences: physics, geology, mathematics, chemistry ....
S L = secretarial. Interest in office and clerical matters. Filing papers, organizing, correspondence ....
S P = sport. Active participation in sports and athletics, whether outdoor (e.g. cricket) or indoor (e.g. boxing) ....
T = travel. Visiting new places, including going abroad. Geographical interests ....
Z = any other specially keen interests. (Give them in the space below)

nized to overlap very considerably. The distinction between *Outdoor activities* (*O*) and *Sport* (*SP*) may at first sight appear to be somewhat arbitrary. A glance at their descriptions in Table I, however, reveals that the latter is concerned mainly with competitive sports whilst the former virtually excludes these but does tend to include appreciative awareness of one's outdoor surroundings. Occasional, but infrequent, overlap is found between *Outdoor* interests (e.g. PASS → 'mountain') and *Agricultural* interests (e.g. BAIL/BALE → 'hay').

It may be seen that Table I contains a few unusual interests for which the Brook had not originally been intended to cater. For example, *Military* (*M*) and *Legal* (*LW*) feature – not because these are considered to be particularly important – but because their inclusion allows for the classification of a substantial minority of responses (such as 'army horse' to GRAZE/GREYS and 'law court' to ARTICLE) which would otherwise have had to be categorized as *Unclassifiable* (*UN*). The score-ranges of these two categories (*M* and *LW*) are very limited, however, and their frequency distributions are skewed – as opposed to the majority of the other interest categories, most of which approach normality (*see* note [B]). Certain other interests which crop up occasionally in the responses, such as household possessions, the Royal Family and domestic pets, are not catered for in the Brook, such responses being classified as *UN*. The aim is to include all those interest categories which have diagnostic importance, vocationally and educationally.

The test itself consists of eighty stimulus words. They were selected on account of their ambiguity and they were considered to be emotionally neutral words: they all have two or more distinct meanings, which are related to two or more of the interests covered by the test. Stimulus words which it was thought might worry, embarrass or antagonize the Subject have been avoided.

The majority of the Subjects manage to hear most of the stimuli correctly but a few are sometimes misheard, e.g. SAIL/SALE is sometimes heard as SANE or SAME, PLOT as CLOT, SEW/SOW/ SO as SOUL/SOLE. The policy of scoring responses to misheard stimulus words, has amply justified itself. There may well often be relevant psychological reasons for the particular mishearing; moreover, conveniently, many of the mishearings are themselves ambiguous words. The eighty stimuli are always presented in the same order, since it has been established that no mental set is induced as a result of the order in which the stimuli are given.[4] The tape-recording ensures uniformity of instructions, accent, speed, intonation, etc. It is essential that the test be given orally because of differences in spelling among some of the stimulus words, e.g. PEAK/PEKE/PIQUE/PEEK.

Four points are scored for each response. Thus, since there are eighty stimulus words, each Subject obtains a grand total of 320 points. A response which consists of at least two words and is all of a piece, as in the answers to CANVAS given on page 99, will score four points on one interest category. For instance, 'oils painting Picasso' scores *Aesthetic* 4 and 'tent camping countryside stream' scores *Outdoor* 4. But when a Subject responds, say, to two different meanings of the stimulus word, the four points are divided between those two meanings. For example, someone who writes in reply to ACT → 'theatre Apostles' would score two for *Entertainment* and two for *Religious*. One who writes 'tent pole election' in reply to CANVAS would split his scores between *Outdoor* and *Political* but, as has been shown, it is not necessary for a Subject to produce either a Multiple Theme or a play on words in order to split his score between two or more categories. CELL/SELL → 'battery' would split between *Practical* and *Physical Sciences;* SCALES → 'justice' would split between *Legal* and *Intellectual*. It is thus recognized that certain categories, and certain responses, may span more than one interest.

If at least two response words are given, there are four points to dispose of and these may be allocated in any way between one, two, three or four interest categories. Additional points are not gained for responses of three or more words, since it was thought undesirable that the slower writer should automatically appear to have fewer or shallower interests than the faster writer. A Subject who responds with only one word is regarded as having *Missed Out* a word and this is recorded as *MO*. Thus, for instance, someone who gave 'music' alone, in reply to the stimulus word KEY/QUAY, would score $A2$, $MO2$. Whereas if he gave 'door' alone to the same stimulus, he would score $UN2$, $MO2$. A complete blank is scored $MO4$.

It may be recalled that responses which do not fit neatly into any one, or any combination, of the twenty-two interest categories are designated as *Unclassifiable*. Examples of such responses would be: ANGLE → 'corner room', $UN4$; JOINT → 'stiff tight loose', $UN4$; CELL/SELL → 'shop street lamp-posts', $B2$, $UN2$. In the last example, two points are awarded for *Business*, since the Subject took the *selling* meaning of CELL/SELL but the rest of the response neither follows up the financial implications (as does, for instance, 'buy distribute eat', scoring $B3$, $F1$) nor goes into the question of what is sold in the shop – which might have yielded a further interest as, for instance, in 'buy clothes material' in reply to the same stimulus, and scoring $B2$, $C2$.

By the inclusion of the UNs and the MOs, a system of scoring is achieved which is non-ipsative (*see* Note [O]), i.e. an identical amount of 'interestability' for all is not assumed by the Brook. It is possible to produce a test profile indicating interests which are broad and deep or which are narrow and superficial – or, of course, the Subject may produce one of the profiles which are more familiar in traditional tests of personal interests, namely the sort indicating broad interests which are comparatively shallow or the sort indicating few, these few being rather deep. As far as the twenty-two interests are concerned, the Brook can produce an almost infinite variety of test results.

The majority of the interest scores produce near-normal frequency distributions [B] – *Military* and *Legal* being marked exceptions, as mentioned on page 102. No attempt has been made, however, either to reduce the frequency distributions to normality or to equate the mean score on all interests. The mean scores are indeed very far from being identical. For instance, on sailors' norms, the means for *Literary*, *Practical* and *Aesthetic* are, respectively 3·2, 19·1 and 6·7. For grammar school girls, the means on the same three interest categories are, respectively,

6·4, 13·9 and 10·6. These figures illustrate the possibility of making inter-group comparisons, using the Brook Reaction test.

They give some indication also of the importance of getting out adequate norms before attempting to draw any conclusions from the test results. The establishment of norms ensures that a given score on a given interest is correctly interpreted – being compared with the scores of other Subjects, matched for age and education. It ensures also that the relative popularity of certain senses of the stimulus words is automatically taken into account.

We shall now discuss the Brook as a clinical test of temperament: a test which aids in the recognition of Subjects who are psychiatrically disturbed, or potentially so. The main index contributing to an ominous-looking test result is a high number of *Questionable* (*Q*) responses. These responses are sometimes, additionally, classifiable in terms of one or more of the twenty-two interests and are sometimes *Unclassifiable*. They are responses referring to death, illness, pain or unpleasurable emotions, such as fear or loneliness; other examples of *Q*s are bizarre, aggressive and highly subjective answers. *Questionable* responses are scored as *Q* 2 if they are severe (e.g. CHORD/CORD → 'hanging noose murder'; SERVICE → 'bad misery loneliness'); and as *Q* 1 if they are mild (e.g. PASS → 'speed 40 mph Jaguar crash'; CARVING → 'joint knee water').

All *Q* responses are classified as one of twelve types. In the illustrations just given, for instance, the response to CHORD would be categorized as *Q* 2, *aggressive* and the response to SERVICE as *Q* 2, *emotion*. The other two would be classified, respectively, as *Q* 1, *calamity* and *Q* 1, *physical illness*. Owing to the blandness of the stimulus words, *Q* responses are the exception rather than the rule. It was this rarity, combined with the fact of subsequent psychiatric breakdown on the part of some givers of a high number of *Q*s, that led us to investigate the hypothesis that such responses may be psychologically significant.

The majority of high *Q* responses are given by a small minority of Subjects. The phenomenon of *Questionable* responses is especially intriguing in view of the choice of stimulus words, thought to be neutral and innocuous – unlike many of the previous lists of words selected for word-association tests, which were often chosen for their startling or provocative qualities.[5] Despite the blandness of the Brook stimuli for most Subjects, however, not one of the eighty stimulus words has failed to produce some *Questionable* responses. It is felt that in the Brook Reaction, the horror, or anxiety, or eroticism of the stimulus word is in the ear of the listener and is, therefore, the more likely to be diagnostic.

Eroticism is mentioned here because a second index which appears to be useful as an aid to recognizing the psychologically disturbed Subject is the overtly *sexual* response (X). MODEL → 'bed girl-friend lovely' (from a male Subject) scores $X 2$; KEY → 'chastity virtue misery' (from a female Subject) scores $X 2$ – as well as $Q 1$, *emotion*. The X index is the only one for which scoring sometimes differs between male and female Subjects. Some responses, however, score X for both sexes, e.g. BANK → 'notes fingering sex-play', $X 2$ and COURT/CAUGHT → 'woo witch where when why', $X 1$ (since the Subject evidently assumed the 'courting' sense of the stimulus word).

The remaining indices which look potentially useful on the clinical side are *Multiple Themes* (MT), *Unclassifiable* responses (UN) and *Omissions* (MO). These do not, in isolation, go significantly with instability but their addition to the other criteria appears to increase the significance of the relationship.[6] These, like the other psychiatric indices, were discovered empirically from the testing of young adults (largely students) and of a group of 101 schoolboys. The latter were divided into four subgroups, on the basis of confidential pen-pictures supplied by members of the school staff.

This subgrouping was done by psychologists who did not know the boys' Brook test results. The subgroups were, respectively, (*a*) 'maladjusted' ($n = 12$), (*b*) 'shy and reserved' ($n = 13$), (*c*) 'highly sexed' ($n = 7$) and (*d*) control ($n = 70$). The last subgroup consisted of boys who did not fall into any of the other three subgroups. (One boy came both in subgroup *a* and subgroup *c*). A significant relationship was found between the boys in the subgroups and relevant Brook scores, e.g. high $UN +$

$M O$ for the 'shy and reserved', high X score for the 'highly sexed' and high on all indices combined – especially, high on Q score – for the 'maladjusted'.

In addition to these data, a good deal of evidence on the psychiatric value of the five indices is accumulating, provided partly by university students whose tutors believe them to be well when tested but who subsequently develop psychiatric problems, and partly by patients from mental hospitals and their controls. Thus it is chiefly by means of criterion groups (*see* Chapter 12, pp. 119–20) that the Brook has been validated as a clinical test of temperament.

The same method has been used for validating the Brook as a test of interests. When this technique is combined with correlations between the Brook score and personal ratings (made on the Rating Sheet shown in Table I), statistically significant validatory evidence is available for twenty of the twenty-two interests – the two exceptions being *Entertainment* and *Legal*. The criterion groups for interest validation comprise such groups as architecture/non-architecture students – the former scoring more highly on *Aesthetic* interest; investment research/non-investment research workers – the former scoring more highly on *Business* interest; secretaries/non-secretaries (members of both groups being young women) – the former scoring more highly on *Secretarial* interest; undergraduates/sailors of undergraduate age – the former scoring more highly on *Intellectual*; members of college teams/non-members of college teams – the former scoring more highly on *Sport*; and so on.

The Rating Sheet (*see* Table I) was, in the early days of the Brook, completed by all Subjects, that is, they rated themselves on each interest, after having taken the test. In addition to these self-ratings, the Subjects got at least one other person to rate them independently, usually a friend or a relative. The self-rating has always been given a weighting of fifty per cent, the other one or more ratings making up the remaining fifty per cent. Thus it was the *mean rating* which was compared with the Brook scores and these comparisons were found to yield satisfactorily close connexions for the majority of the interest categories. [1]

So much for validation; now for consistency. The Brook data on consistency comprise two studies, one based on the method of test-retest, the other based on the split-half technique. Investigations into Brook consistency on the assessment of both temperament and interests was considered doubly necessary in view of the suggestion sometimes made that orectic measures are intrinsically likely to prove unreliable and that if any acceptable level of reliability is to be achieved, it is essential to use the method of multiple choice.

In the first of the studies, one hundred university students of both sexes were tested in October and retested in the following June. Product moment correlations (*see* note [1]) were calculated for each of the twenty-two interest categories and for the five measures of temperament. This yielded a total of twenty-seven correlation coefficients of which twenty-four were significant at the 0·05 level of confidence or better, fifteen of them reaching a significance level of 0·001 (*see* note [1]).

In the second study on consistency, carried out by Kline, the Subjects were sixty students in a College of Education.[7] The scores on the first forty items were correlated with the scores on the last forty and the correlations were then corrected for length by the Spearman-Brown formula. The twenty-seven corrected correlations were all over 0·7, the majority of them being over 0·8. Kline makes two comments about his findings. (*a*) 'These reliabilities are almost as high as those of the Strong Vocational Interests Blank and the Kuder Preference Record', both of which are multiple-choice in form. (*b*) 'Although all these [Brook correlations] are substantially high, it would be hard to claim that the two halves of each scale are identical. Thus it would certainly not suffice to give one half of the test alone. Indeed from these figures it is clear that all eighty items are necessary to make the scales reliable.' The present writer is in complete agreement with Kline on this point.

In view of the highly selected nature of the samples in both studies, and the notorious inconsistency of orectic tests, these results are considered quite satisfactory.

It would appear then that the Brook Reaction test has the

requisite consistency as a test both of personal interests and of certain measures of temperament. It appears to have adequate validity in terms of interests and it looks promising from a clinical viewpoint, but further research on its strictly clinical value is indicated. This will probably take the form of testing groups of psychiatric patients (with different diagnoses) alongside control groups of 'normal' Subjects (i.e. people who are not receiving, and have never received, psychiatric treatment) matched for age, sex and education. If the test fulfils its early promise, it will have a variety of uses, vocational, educational and clinical.

What are the drawbacks of the Brook test? There are quite a few. First, the scoring demands both time and skill. Either special training or a very careful perusal of the Brook Manual[8] is required if the scoring is to be done correctly by somebody without previous experience of the test. The scoring is less subjective and less laborious than is that of projective tests but it nonetheless needs a good deal of time, care, insight and knowledge – knowledge not only of the Brook test but wide general knowledge, including for instance the latest slang terms and pop-idioms – if the responses of young people are to be correctly interpreted.

Secondly, the Brook is not suitable for everybody. A fair degree of literacy and of writing speed is required of the Subjects, if the test is to be given in its group form. It would probably not be suitable as it stands for young children (apart from the fact that norms are not available for them) or for people who write with difficulty. The test might of course be given individually to such Subjects and their spoken responses could be recorded. As yet, however, there is no evidence as to whether this would materially change the Subject's responses to the stimuli.

Thirdly, as already mentioned, there are a number of interests which occasionally appear in the test protocols and which are not catered for on the Brook. Examples of these would be smoking, domestic animals and love of material possessions such as cars, houses and household goods – indeed there is no category for the essential home-lover. Fourthly, it is not, and never will be, amenable to machine scoring – though it is an open question whether any test which purports to reflect the infinite variety of human personality could ever be reduced to machine scoring without losing more than is gained.

Finally, there is the question of leg-pulling. The Brook looks as though it offers ample scope for this and many Subjects ask after testing whether we suffer from it. The answer is that we do not in fact know. But a substantial amount of leg-pulling would appear unlikely in view of the good validation and consistency that the test has yielded. Perhaps the answer lies in the shortness of the time allowed for responding to the stimulus word. Some responses are indeed fantastic and far-ranging – but to be fantastic *and* untrue to oneself in twelve seconds is perhaps a near-impossible feat. As Professor Pear points out[9]: if a patient fakes a dream, in order to lead on his psychiatrist, the latter is content that the invention 'proceeds from the patient's own mind'.

The Brook Reaction test is still young. It appears, however, to be healthy and vigorous. So far, it seems to be fulfilling its promise of providing an open-ended test which is fun to take and reasonably objective to score, and which provides results that correlate with other (non-psychometric) measures of personal interests and temperament.

12   The Paradox of Validation

They talk of some strict testing of us – pish! – OMAR KHAYYÁM

The paradox of validation – Personal judgement – Examinations –
Chronological age – Sociological criteria – Prediction – Criterion
groups – Factor analysis – Construct validation – Inter-test
correlations

Psychological testing is based on a paradox. If there is a valid
criterion of, for instance, intelligence, why use an intelligence
test? But there is no perfect criterion so we must make use of
intelligence tests. But how then can we validate the tests? –
against personal judgements, academic examinations, chronological age (for children), occupation and socio-economic status
(for adults), predictive capacity, criterion groups, factor analysis,
construct validation and other tests.

It is generally agreed that each of these criteria has its drawbacks and that none is ideal for validating an intelligence test
since none can be equated with intelligence. Yet most people who
have had much to do with the intelligence test – however sceptical
they may have been at the outset – come to believe that it is the
best single means of appraising someone's cognitive capacity,
the most reliable, in every sense, the least contaminated by
acquired knowledge (on the part of the Subject) and by prejudice
(on the part of the appraiser). They believe that, over the years,
the well-constructed intelligence test has proved itself to be a
useful and a fair guide as to how the individual will react when
faced with a situation demanding a grasp of essentials and an
appropriate response.

This, then, is the paradox to be discussed: the fact (already
referred to earlier) that a good intelligence test is deemed to be
a good method of assessing intelligence in the absence of certain proof and, moreover, that it is deemed to be *better than*
any of the criteria which have been invoked in an endeavour to

establish that proof. Let us first examine some of these criteria.

Personal judgement has been used since time immemorial for assessing the intelligence of others and will no doubt always be so used. Sometimes the judgement is made in an interview, which may be as short as twenty minutes, or even less. It is generally held – and has indeed been demonstrated – that this method is highly unreliable. The interviewer is often inconsistent, assessing a group of Subjects quite differently if he is rash enough to re-interview them on another occasion. It is clear then that he will by no means always agree with other interviewers. He is liable to be influenced by trivial irrelevancies in the Subject's manner or conduct, of whose existence he (the interviewer) may not even be aware. He is apt, for instance, to be very favourably impressed if the Subject laughs at his jokes in the interview – and whilst it may indeed be a matter of intelligence to recognize these as such, failure to register amusement may be due to pride or nervousness in the Subject and not to any lack of intelligence.

The main difficulties in the way of appraising intelligence by means of an interview are twofold. Firstly, the interviewer tends to rate the Subject's intelligence in accordance with how well the two get on together. Secondly, halo effect [R] plays an important part in the assessing of intelligence – as in assessing any other quality by means of personal judgement. These two difficulties are related to each other but they are not identical. It is hard to do anything about them even if one is aware of them. In fact, awareness of them often leads to the phenomenon of 'leaning over backwards' and this probably does not add to the soundness of the method.

Interviewers vary greatly in their personality and their technique – and in their intelligence. Most of them will agree in general that the interview is a tricky instrument, subject to vagaries in the all-important, artificial relationship which is temporarily established, and that it is extraordinarily difficult to assess the Subject with any degree of accuracy. But, on the other hand, many interviewers seem to feel that to them, personally, has been vouchsafed the knack of infallible interviewing. 'There isn't so much that I can do well,' they may assert, with a modest smile, challenging their listener to contest this statement, 'but I *can* interview'. If one has the hardihood to enquire how they do it, and how they know that their assessments are correct, one obtains some such reply as 'Oh, experience you know,' or 'Well, it's a gift, I suppose, like any other.'

Personal judgement of the Subject's degree of intelligence based on long-standing acquaintance with him is slightly less risky than that based on the interview. There are certain other difficulties here, however.

One, interestingly enough, is the degree of intelligence of the judge. It has been found, in research on teachers' assessments of school children, that the highly intelligent teachers are far better able to appraise their pupils' ability than are the less intelligent teachers,[1] i.e. teachers with high intelligence scores differentiate among their pupils more finely, and more clearly in accordance with the pupils' test scores, than do teachers who score lower on an intelligence test. A second difficulty is the fact that the judges, whoever they may be, inevitably have varying standards – some higher, some lower. It is therefore desirable to have as many Subjects as possible rated by the same judge. But if the same person has to judge dozens, or even hundreds, of individuals, it is unlikely that he can know them very well. If, on the other hand, there are few Subjects and he does know them very well he is liable to be partial – in one direction or the other. The longer and better two individuals know each other, the more personally entangled they are likely to become. This is not usually compatible with the clear, detached judgement which is required for the purpose of assessment.

Personal judgement will surely continue to be used, however, when an appraisal of someone is necessary. There are circumstances in which this is virtually the only possible method and, as will be seen, it enters into many of the other criteria which are used in attempts to validate intelligence tests. It enters very obviously into academic examinations, which have also been used over the years. Indeed, the latter have so frequently been employed as a criterion that many psychologists and school-teachers prefer to speak nowadays of tests of 'scholastic aptitude' rather than of 'intelligence'. This is partly because these tests of reasoning are often used in England and the U.S.A. as an aid to educational selection and allocation and partly because, in some contexts, 'intelligence' has become a pejorative word: people tend to be less offended at being asked to take part in a test of 'scholastic aptitude' than in a test of 'intelligence'. As was shown, however, during World War II,[2] for instance, tests of reasoning – however they may be named – can be helpful in determining appropriate level of job, manual or clerical or mechanical: the uses of the intelligence test are not in fact confined to the schoolroom and the university.

Academic examinations at all levels from seven-year-olds up have been employed as criteria for intelligence test validation. A great deal of work has been done in England, following up the 11+ testings into the fifth and sixth forms of grammar schools;[3] and an enormous amount has been done in the U.S.A. at College level. A battery of cognitive tests has to be taken as a matter of routine by every would-be student at an American college or university.[4] From the point of view of test-validation these data are always less than satisfactory because of the restricted range of the groups tested. Since the test results are used as an aid to selection (for grammar schools or university) only Subjects who do well on the tests are in fact selected. The unselected then have a different sort of education and cannot be followed up in the same way. Thus any correlation found between those selected for higher education and the results they finally gain (whether in G.C.E. or in their degree examinations) are likely to be lower than they would be, had this selection not taken place.

Many psychometrists 'correct for homogeneity' but I dislike this practice, as do many statisticians. Since it is legitimate to 'correct' either for selection, as described above, or for internal inconsistency in the test used – 'attenuation' [5] – it is possible artificially to step up the validity correlation coefficient of a given test to a considerable, and misleading, extent. In my view, it is preferable to produce tests suited in difficulty for the superior group who will be followed up – i.e. tests yielding near-chance scores among non-members – and to give the straightforward correlation, unraised by 'correction'. If it is felt that this uncorrected correlation fails to do justice to the test's validity, it is always possible to add an explanatory note to that effect.

There are other grounds for objection besides attenuation, to using academic examinations as a means of validating intelligence tests. An academic examination usually asks for information on some highly specific topic, such as history or chemistry, whereas the typical intelligence test aims to be general and to steer clear of factual information as far as possible. A good examination result depends partly on the industry of the candidate, the excellence of his memory and of his health over the years, the way he was taught and the extent to which he got on with his teacher (or, perhaps, his teaching-machine). By design, these factors play a negligible part in determining the Subject's intelligence test score. In fact, most examiners would say that intelligence is necessary, but not sufficient, to do well in their examinations.

Thus, whilst one would expect a positive correlation between examinations and intelligence tests, a very close relationship is not to be expected. And a positive, but not very high, correlation is precisely what is found in most such cases. The extent of the relationship varies: (a) with the test used, verbally biased tests predictably tallying more closely with examination results than do diagrammatic tests. (b) The relationship varies also with the examination subject, physicists, mathematicians and philosophers, for instance, producing higher correlations (and also higher scores) than do, say, modern linguists and specialists in English literature. There are probably many reasons for this, the most likely being that deductive reasoning plays a far larger role in mathematics and philosophy than it does in languages and literature; and that the scoring of the latter type of examinations is necessarily more subjective than that in the former type.

Binet used chronological age (or, rather, what-the-child-can-do-at-what-age) as his criterion for test validity at the beginning of this century and it has been used, off and on, ever since. At first it seems the ideal criterion since it is objective, independent both of test score and of personal judgement, and there is no doubt that an individual's intelligence does rise from five to fifteen (which was the age range with which Binet was concerned). But, alas, it is not only intelligence which increases over these years. Everything else seems to increase too: height, weight, speed of running, strength of hand-grip, size of ears, mechanical aptitude, pride in personal appearance . . . . It is difficult to think of any mental or physical attribute which does not increase or improve with age, during the period five to fifteen.

It is not, therefore, such a satisfactory criterion as would appear at first sight. Undoubtedly problems requiring intelligence for their solution are tackled more and more competently as the child grows older; and he can succeed in tasks at ten which he failed at eight, and at fifteen which he failed at thirteen. But this is absolutely no guarantee that the problems involved are necessarily testing *intelligent* activity, however this be defined or described. In fact, considerable ingenuity would be required to devise problems which are solved as well at an early age as they are at a later age (within the five-to-fifteen period). After the late teens, no psychometrist would think of using age as a criterion since, as is well-known, tested intelligence reaches a plateau in early adulthood and begins its slow decline usually in the thirties, if not sooner. This gloomy finding is discussed in Chapter 13.

It is clear, then, that chronological age cannot be used as the criterion for adults. Occupation has sometimes been chosen for adults and, related to this, socio-economic status. A number of large-scale investigations have been conducted in which the intelligence test result and the job of thousands of Subjects (e.g. tested in the Services in war-time) are recorded, and a comparison made between the two.[5] The mean test score is calculated for members of each occupation – university professor, general practitioner, salesman, semi-skilled industrial worker, general labourer, etc. – and the order of these means has sometimes been taken as a kind of validation of the test.

Four points are worth making about these enquiries. (*a*) The order is usually roughly in accordance with common-sense assumptions. For instance, the mean scores for the five jobs mentioned in the preceding paragraph would occur in the order given therein – along with the dozens of other jobs, whose means fit in between the professors at the top and the labourers at the bottom. But (b) there is a very considerable degree of overlap, not only between adjacent rungs of the ladder but between rungs several steps away. (c) The range of score for each job differs tremendously, but it differs also systematically: the further down the ladder we look, the wider the range obtaining among members of the occupation. General practitioners, for instance, yield a wider range of test score than do professors but the scores of the former are still confined within a fairly narrow range. When we reach the bottom rung, and look at the range of scores found among labourers, this is exceedingly wide, indicating far more tolerance – or should we say far more waste?

These findings are probably related to point (d), namely that the investigators have simply taken the people in their jobs and calculated the relevant mean scores. This implies the assumption that all round pegs are inevitably fitted into round holes, as things are at present; that square pegs are equally comfortably fitted into square holes; and that even the occasional irregular hexagon is fitted neatly into his appropriate hexagonal hole. No enquiries have been made into the success of the Subjects in their respective jobs nor into the degree of satisfaction enjoyed by the Subjects in their work. It would be difficult and laborious to ascertain these data but it would be well worthwhile attempting to do so. Such an enquiry might be of general psychological interest and might also yield acceptable evidence for test-validation – though it should be remembered that intelligence testing can yield data regarding *level* of appropriate job only; it has little to offer regarding *type* of work, at any given level.

Socio-economic status has been used by some psychologists and sociologists as a further criterion. For example, the social class of the Subject (or his parents, in the case of a child) has been compared with intelligence test score; as has also been the income earned by the Subject (or his parent). Again the statistical results are as would be predicted: on the whole, those in higher-level social classes and salary-classes gain higher intelligence test scores than do those in the lower echelons. This criterion, too, is open to objection.

Let us confine ourselves here to the two most obvious. First, any finding as to social status and intelligence test score raises the question of how far the test assesses innate capacity and how far its results are influenced by the environment of the Subject. Is he 'upper class' because he is bright? Or is he bright because he is 'upper class'? Secondly, salary level is obviously a grossly inadequate criterion since people's interests vary; some people prefer lowly-paid work which they enjoy to more highly-paid work which they find uninteresting. It is not the case that the most highly-paid posts are necessarily those demanding the greatest intellectual ability. Moreover, there is some evidence that a 'business sense' and money-making ability are highly specific aptitudes, closely related to interest in this field, perhaps not always so closely related to intelligence.

The predictive capacity of intelligence tests is open to many of the same objections. Several psychologists have tested the intelligence of young children and have then made a longitudinal study by following them through school days, through adolescence, through college (where applicable) and into their early, and even later, careers. This has been done both in the U.S.A. and in the U.K. One of the best known of these investigations is Terman's study of gifted children.[6] In the early 1920s he selected 1,000 children who had IQs over 140. He and his colleagues then followed up these gifted children throughout their lives, many of whom are now grandparents. Terman compared them every few years with Controls, who were representative of the total population, and he found that the members of his original gifted group were ahead all the way. Life apparently smiled upon them. They had better physical and mental health than the Controls; were better athletes as well as better scholars; they won the prizes, the scholarships and the positions of responsibility; they produced relatively few delinquents and criminals; they took out more patents and wrote more books; they had happier marriages, better jobs and higher incomes; their children and grandchildren tended to follow the same pattern.

Others who have made longitudinal surveys based primarily on I.Q. have produced comparable results. These results cannot be laughed off but again one is forced to examine such criteria as 'better jobs' and 'higher incomes'. It is terribly easy to over-simplify these issues: they are indeed far from simple. While not wishing to disparage the person with the high I.Q. who fits comfortably into society, comes up with all the right answers in all the right contexts and is regarded by many as the salt of the earth, one should not ignore the occasional uncompromising individualist who refuses to fall into line, who adopts perhaps an irregular, ill-paid way of life – and who may be highly intelligent, but 'doesn't fit in', partly by reason of his temperament and partly because of his quality of mind. We have already suggested that these two are basically inseparable.

The next method, that of criterion groups, is rather like the method of longitudinal study in reverse. When validating by criterion groups, instead of testing his Subjects in infancy, following them through and seeing in what groups they finish, the psychologist selects certain groups whom he believes to be clearly differentiated from one another intelligence-wise. This is an extension of Thorndike's 'first approximation' to a definition of intelligence.[7] 'Let intellect be defined as that quality of mind (or brain or behaviour if one prefers) in respect to which Aristotle, Plato, Thucydides, and the like, differed most from Athenian idiots of their day, or in respect to which the lawyers, physicians, scientists, scholars, and editors of reputed greatest ability at constant age, say a dozen of each, differ most from idiots of that age in our asylums.' Thorndike offered this as a definition of intellect; it is also a very clear account of the method of criterion groups. First catch your group; then test it; then see whether the score gained by group X is, as predicted, higher than the score gained by Group Y and, if so, whether the predicted difference is significant.

It is of course desirable that the groups to be compared should not have been selected at any stage *by means of* an intelligence test – and this condition is becoming difficult to fulfil. For example, to compare thirteen-year-old secondary modern school children with thirteen-year-old grammar school children on a test would not be acceptable, since their initial segregation was effected partly on the basis of an intelligence test. Moreover, the different training they will have had since they moved to their respective secondary schools, will tend to reinforce any intellectual differences between the two groups.

On the other hand, the comparison of professional men with idiots, as Thorndike suggests, although acceptable as a 'first approximation' to a definition scarcely offers a fine enough distinction for validating a new test. If the gap between the two extremes can be filled, and the various groups be known not to have been selected in the first place by means of an intelligence test, this is a promising method of intelligence test validation. It is, incidentally, a method which is used in sorting test items, the criterion groups then being the high scorers on the test as a whole, as compared with the low scorers on the test as a whole.

This internal dependence on the test itself brings us to the last three methods of test validation: factor analysis, construct validation and correlations with different tests. The other validation techniques discussed above depend on criteria external to the tests. This seems to me to be an advantage although, as has been shown, none of the methods is ideal. Factor analysis, construct validation and inter-test correlation lack the advantage of test-independence but they lack also some of the drawbacks of the other methods: they are capable of quantitative expression and they are considered by many psychometrists to be 'pure' and 'objective'. But this last claim is controversial.

Let us take factor analysis first [J]. This is a method which the present writer has discussed at some length in a previous book.[8] It is a technique which involves administering a good many tests to a large number of Subjects, calculating the correlations between every pair of tests in the battery and extracting 'factors', by any one of various methods, from the inter-correlations so obtained. Such factors may be given such names as verbal fluency or numeracy or conscientiousness. Their number and variety are immense and evergrowing. The results, i.e. the kind and the number of 'factors extracted' in any one experiment depend on the particular method favoured, the tests used; the groups selected and, of course, the psychological acumen and predilections of the particular factor analyst, since he often gives subjectively meaningful names to the alleged factors. As Sir Godfrey Thomson said long ago[9]: '... the analysis is not unique ... innumerable alternative analyses are possible, all fulfilling the experimental conditions'.

Factor analysis is perhaps a useful method of test *classification* – although it is arguable that the grouping of the various tests can generally be determined by inspection of the matrix of intercorrelations plus inspection of the content of the tests in the first place. But, in the writer's opinion, one cannot ascertain 'the structure of the mind' or the 'hierarchy of mental factors' or 'the nature of intelligence' by means of factor analysis – partly for the reasons stated in the preceding paragraph and partly because such phrases imply a rigidity and simplicity which is inapplicable. Nonetheless, most of the work done in the field of psychological testing over the last few decades has been in terms of factor analysis; most of the arguments have been about the rival merits of varying types of factor analysis; and many factor analysts evidently believe – despite the internal nature of the evidence – that they hold the key to the problem of test validation as well as test classification.

Construct validation is not identifiable with factor analysis although, for some psychologists, the two appear to be intimately related. Professor P. E. Vernon writes, for instance that:[10]

The most appropriate approach in such circumstances is known as *Construct Validation*. By this is implied that the psychologist designs a test to measure a certain hypothetical quality or 'construct' and, in the absence of satisfactory external validation, seeks indirect evidence that the theory underlying his test is sound. Thus Spearman put forward the *g* factor as a theory to explain the correlations among varied cognitive tests, and was able to show by factor analysis that tests involving abstraction and other higher intellectual processes were highly saturated with *g*.

And again:[11]

Construct validation implies testing out the theory underlying the test, or determining the psychological meaning of the test score. For example, if 'sociability' is a measurable construct, there should be factorial consistency.

Along similar, though not identical, lines, Professor Butcher writes:[12]

Construct validity is a measure of the extent to which a test actually represents the intended construct, such as intelligence. It is the most important kind and the most difficult to establish; the most important because it is, at least in principle, free from the arbitrariness that applies to the other types, and because it is closest in conception to the intuitive idea of validity as the degree to which the test fulfils its purpose. It is just this that makes construct validity difficult to establish....

In general the notion of construct validity implies an 'open-ended' view. Construct validity is a kind of second-order concept in which the evidence, for instance, of concurrent and predictive validities may be taken into account. A quantitative measure of construct validity again is not easy to obtain, except by factor analysis. This is an important exception, however, since if one makes the required assumptions, factor analysis provides the only kind of validation that is not tied to a particular arbitrary criterion.

On the other hand, according to Cronbach,[13]

Whenever a tester asks what a score means psychologically or what causes a person to get a certain test score, he is asking what concepts may properly be used to interpret the test performance. This type of theoretical concept is called a construct validation. In order to show that a given construct applies to a test, it is necessary to derive hypotheses about test behaviour from the theory related to the construct and to verify them experimentally.

It may be seen that this last statement does not necessarily make any factorial implications. These excerpts from three authorities may indicate the reasons for the present writer's reluctance to give her own account of construct validity. Quotations have been used in order to demonstrate the difficulty of attaining any clear understanding of the term, to suggest that its connotation is subjective and that the term is used, typically, to apply to tests of temperament rather than to exclusively cognitive tests. In note [T] two further statements are given – again authoritatively but discordantly – on the topic of construct validation.

Let us turn with relief to the simpler, less controversial, next (and last) method of validation, namely that of straightforward inter-test correlation. The argument for this method is as follows. The best way of assessing intelligence is clearly by means of an intelligence test. This is what intelligence tests are for and there is no other instrument so well equipped for this function. There-fore, equally clearly, the best way of validating a new intelligence test is by seeing how well it tallies with an already well-established intelligence test, i.e. by correlating the new test with an old one. If the correlation is high, then the new test is also a good one. This sounds sensible; indeed it is sensible provided (*a*) that this inter-test correlation technique is not used in isolation and (*b*) that the 'well-established' earlier test is really well-established, that is, convincingly validated – and this is where we came in!

It is my view that a good intelligence test is genuinely the best single means of appraising someone's present functioning cogni-tive capacity, in relation to that of other people. Hence it follows that one of the best methods of validating a new test is by means of correlating it with an earlier reputable test. It must be borne in mind that many tests on the market are *not* reputable; and also that if changes are made in the new test (and there are signs at last of some changes in the methods that have been doggedly followed over the last fifty years) such changes may reduce the level of agreement between the new test and the old.

This technique of validation is obviously open to the charge of circularity. Yet it is often claimed to be one of the best means of test validation and it is often claimed that intelligence testing is a valuable, irreplaceable process. How do these two claims square? And how does the latter claim square with the defects attributed, above, to all the other techniques of test validation? The answer lies in the over-all, global results; in the repeated finding that whatever criterion is chosen, it tends to go with test results; that in general, the test score confirms the past and the future – and that where it fails to confirm, the test score often throws further light on some problem, especially when the test score is unexpectedly high. As indicated in Chapter 2, discrepancies are the exception rather than the rule, and where discrepancies are found the intelligence test is likely to prove particularly useful. The validation is usually a statistical or actuarial matter; the discrepancy is usually concerned with an individual.

This chapter has dealt almost exclusively with the validation of tests of intelligence. Other cognitive tests – those of specific aptitudes – present somewhat less of a problem since it is often possible to validate these against certain relevant skills, acquired to a greater or lesser degree some time after the aptitude test has been taken. On the other hand, the validation of tests of temperament and character presents a well-nigh intractable problem. Most psychologists who use these tests seem tacitly to have given up the struggle. They announce that they will use their relevant term purely operationally – be it 'anxiety' or 'introversion' or 'radicalism' and, sure enough, it transpires that the so-called 'anxious person', for instance, is simply somebody who has scored highly on a self-styled 'test of anxiety'. What is unacceptable here is the employment of terms which have a definite, non-psychometric meaning both for the layman and the psychiatrist. Sometimes psychiatric assessments, based on clinical interview, are used as the external criterion. But these – in addition to covering a rather limited field – often conflict with one another.

To sum up: there is little room for complacency on the matter of test-validation. Indeed a frank expression of unease would probably be healthier than the current fashion of ignoring the monster. For example, a recent book on intelligence and ability,[14] does not even mention validity or validation once in its index (or in its text) although the book deals largely with psychological testing, and this is surely one of the most fundamental concepts in this field. Moreover, in this respect, the book is not unique.

The validation of cognitive tests to date is defensible, however, when one takes a bird's eye view. It is based on a paradox but at least it is a stable paradox. The lack of acceptable test validity in the orectic field is due largely to the unsatisfactory nature of most of the orectic tests, themselves. That there is hope for better things has optimistically been suggested, in Chapter 11.

13 Intelligence Test Score and Ageing

When the age is in, the wit is out – SHAKESPEARE

Intelligence test score and ageing – Importance of type of test used – Peak age of achievement – Psychological differences between the generations

It used to be stated in the text-books that intelligence developed swiftly in infancy and childhood, more slowly in early adolescence, and that its development ceased at about fifteen years of age. When the intelligence testing movement was itself young and immature, some psychologists even put this abrupt halt as early as fourteen. It is now realized, however, that this apparent full-stop in mid-adolescence was illusory and was due partly to the inadequacy of the tests used and partly to the lack of education, and of intellectual opportunity, which afflicted the majority of the population.

The tests were inadequate because they were insufficiently difficult and insufficiently interesting. They did not provide much in the way of intellectual stimulation or challenge. The intelligent young person was liable to feel contemptuous of the test problems; he got a good many items right; but he *did not have the scope* to improve at seventeen or eighteen on the performance he had achieved at fifteen or sixteen.

In addition to the failure of the tests to extend these Subjects, comparatively few people had the opportunity to continue their education beyond fifteen years of age. Since, in those days, it was claimed that intelligence tests measured innate endowment and that this is virtually independent of education, the step was easily taken to the bland assertion that these tests prove that innate ability ceases to increase after the middle teens. This is what budding psychologists were taught as fact in the early 1930s. No suggestion was made either that the taking of intelligence tests may be regarded to some extent as a skill which feeds on intellectual practice nor that harder tests might transform the discrimination effected among intelligent young adults.

There has been a marked change in attitude on this point, in recent years, owing (a) to the development of tests of high grade intelligence[1] and (b) to the education explosion of the 1960s. (a) has demonstrated that it is possible to differentiate, intellectually, among highly selected intelligent young adults whose I.Q.s fall within the restricted range of about 125–150. (b) has shown that a far greater proportion of the population than had been thought, can successfully take G.C.E. examinations and can gain university degrees. (a) and (b) jointly have demonstrated that intelligence test scores will often rise from the age of fifteen to the age of seventeen and even eighteen, given that the test offers sufficient scope and that the Subjects are not allowing their intelligence to grow rusty.

The analogy between engineering and psychology does appear to be justified here. From about eighteen to the middle or late twenties, intelligence as tested seems to remain fairly stable among people who use their brains – after which it usually begins its downward trend. But for people who do virtually no reading and thinking, and whose work demands little in the way of reflection, judgement and perception, the descent starts earlier and progresses more steeply. It is difficult, as ever, to disentangle cause and effect, since there is a tendency for the initially brighter to take up work (and play) which is more intellectually demanding and which is therefore liable to delay the process of rusting.

Thus the picture of the rise and fall of an individual's intelligence is roughly that shown in Fig. 1, for Subjects X, Y and Z, X being highly intelligent, Y around average and Z well below average. These three are assumed, in order not to complicate the issue, to have been in occupations well suited to their ability, during their working lives. It will be seen that they retain the same pecking order throughout life; also that X reaches his peak at roughly the same age as Z but holds it considerably longer than Z, his tested intelligence declining far more slowly than Z's. Y's performance lies, throughout, between that of X and that of Z.

This is the picture presented by the majority of intelligence tests. Why should this be? The question concerns not so much the constancy of the relationship between X, Y and Z – since constancy has been 'built into' intelligence tests as far as their devisers have been able to do so – but rather the universal decline.

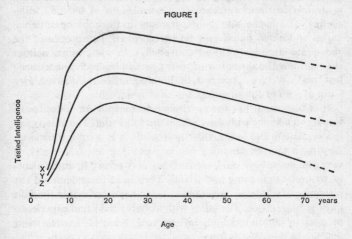

FIGURE 1

Does the picture correspond with 'real life'? We know that the latter is a great deal more blurred and controversial than its psychometric counterpart. Figure 1 thus raises a good many questions for discussion. Does the peak of test-performance not vary with the type of test used? And does it not vary too in different fields of work? Are the middle-aged and elderly really as much dimmer than the young as many of the young would have us believe? Or do they gain in experience, knowledge and wisdom what they lose in reasoning, speed and percipience? How about the close relationship which has been repeatedly stressed in this book between the cognitive and the orectic? Does this hold when changes with age are considered? Let us discuss these various topics beginning with the question as to why tested intelligence exhibits such a marked decline with age.

The decline is clearly physiologically based, as are many mental changes, but in this book we are dealing with the psychological aspect. The latter may well parallel the physiological aspect but it is not the same thing, nor can it be explained (or explained away) in terms of physiology. An experience of toothache, for instance, is not *equivalent to* dental caries, just as seeing a patch of red is not *equivalent to* the occurrence of a wavelength of 0·00062 milli-metres. Toothache may be experienced in the absence of dental caries and a red patch may be perceived in the absence of the 'adequate stimulus' [U] (and conversely). In such cases, neither the pain nor the sensation of seeing something red is necessarily less 'real'. We are concerned, in this chapter, with the *psychology* – not of pain or colour vision, but of growing old.

It is suggested that the psychological reasons for a decline in tested intelligence with age include the following. The elderly are less confident and less highly motivated. It is a long time since they have tackled anything like a reasoning test (they may, if very old, never have done so) and they may regard it, ambivalent-ly, as both frightening and trivial. They need to understand the relevance of what they are asked to do to a greater extent than do most young people. The latter will probably have had experience of tests in childhood and, in any case, what is new for them tends to be regarded as fun.

It has been shown that speed is an asset in intelligence test taking and there is no doubt that the old are slower than the young. This is partly because of a general tendency to slow down, mentally and physically, with age, starting as young as in the late twenties. But it is due also to the fact that experience has taught many older people the value of checking. Speed at any price is a god for many young people whereas for some of the old it is anti-Christ. A further possibility is that the older person has learned to hold something in reserve in case of emergency. He may there-fore be unwilling to push himself, whereas the youngster will tend to go all out – a definite advantage in a short, timed test.

Apart from these changes in attitude, however, there are un-deniable and relevant cognitive changes. The older Subject has less good short-term memory, he often reasons less cogently and is a less acute observer than he was in his youth. All these changes will adversely affect his test performance – and especially his *intelligence* test performance since this is, as we saw in Chapters 2 and 8, the least specific of cognitive tests.

Certain intelligence tests suffer less than others, however, from the process of ageing. Vocabulary tests which have a steep gradient of difficulty are considered to be a good means of assessing intelligence. They correlate highly with other measures – which cannot easily be dismissed as measures of acquired knowledge – and they are included in the two best-known individual intelligence scales, those of Binet[2] and Wechsler,[3] respectively. But vocabulary tests obviously do assess knowledge and this is probably why they are about the only cognitive tests to date which 'hold up' over the years. Indeed vocabulary score may positively rise, up to and beyond middle life, especially among people who spend much of their time in reading and discussion. Other cognitive tests fare less well with the elderly, even when the Subjects have maintained their intellectual interests and activities over the years.

Thus the quantitative assessment of the intellectual calibre of the middle-aged and older presents serious problems. The older the Subject, the greater are the difficulties, for the less appropriate in general are the psychometric measures. Yet such assessment has occasionally to be done, e.g. in vocational guidance for the not-so-young who wish to change their job and for aiding psychiatric diagnosis and therapy. A method of treatment which succeeds with a highly intelligent patient (of whatever age) may well prove useless with a duller patient (of the same age), and conversely. In such cases, the psychiatrist will probably use such psychometric tools as he has, but he may well end by relying mainly on the Subject's life-history to date.

Let us therefore consider real life, as opposed to psychometric findings. There is little doubt that, outside the psychological laboratory, the young are more acute observers, swifter and more cogent reasoners than are their elders. This may be due partly to their superior hearing and vision, their greater interest since more is new to them and, possibly, to their being less cluttered up with ingested ideas, facts and habits. They do not suffer from 'negative transfer' to the same extent as the old [V]. It is therefore to be expected that they should excel in most cognitive tests. They do not have it all their own way, however. This is evident if one considers, for instance, the facts of car-insurance. The greater accident rate of the young is so well-attested (partly owing to their passion for speed, mentioned above) that some insurance companies are loth to accept clients between seventeen and twenty-five years of age, and those that do take them on charge far higher premiums than for members of any other age group. This particular real life advantage of the older adult is not unique. He also fares better on certain methods of industrial retraining.[4]

Such advantages may be exceptional, but it is worth bearing them in mind when theorizing about the psychological effects of ageing and when taking decisions which affect people's lives. The cult of Youth, with a capital Y, is a relatively new phenomenon. It used to be the aged – even the very aged – who were consulted on problems of importance. The older person clearly has, in general, more experience on which to draw and this may improve his judgement, as compared with that of his chronological junior. If, however, the senior *assumes* that his judgement is superior simply by virtue of his having lived longer, this in itself implies a *lack* of judgement. It is all too easy not to learn from experience. The sexagenarian who has retained (or even, perhaps, acquired) some humility probably has the wisdom to offset his incipient senility.

Lest 'incipient senility' be thought to be too strong a term for the average sixty-year-old, it is perhaps worth pointing out that individual differences in the process of ageing are as immense as they are in all other spheres. Some people begin noticeably to slow down and to lose their powers of concentration at fifty, or younger; their memory, both short-term and long-term, is less reliable than it was – with the possible exception of reminiscence of early experiences, which are usually conveniently uncheckable; they may tell the same unfortunate hearer the same story three times in as many weeks; in particular, they suffer from amnesia[W], most obviously in the case of names. Whereas the youngster may have occasional trouble in recalling a name with which he is not very familiar, the elderly and even the middle-aged are constantly groping for names and words which, they justifiably protest, they 'know perfectly well'. Magnify these symptoms: hear the same story told by the same narrator three times in three quarters of an hour; wait patiently while he searches unavailingly for the name of his favourite holiday resort; and it is sadly clear that the picture begins to approximate to that of senility. If there is indeed a distinguishing feature, it lies perhaps in the 'lack of insight' [X] of the truly senile.

What of the question of peak age for achievement? It is surely true that this, and also the typical age for onset of decline, does vary with the field of work. Mathematicians, for instance, are well-known for the extreme youth at which they produce their best work – often before twenty-five.[5] Some composers (notably Mozart) embark very youthfully and successfully on their career; others, such as Stravinsky (who also was successful when young) are still going strong in their eighties. Mozart, himself, might have composed equally well in later life, had he not died in his thirties. Kendall[6] writes controversially on mathematicians and musicians, as compared with statisticians and poets.

Robert Graves somewhere remarks that although musicians are often precocious, poets never are. One can draw the same kind of distinction between mathematicians, who are usually precocious and statisticians who, as statisticians, are not. There is a certain apprenticeship in handling real-life situations to be served before an individual is mature enough to tackle important statistical problems.

In general, it looks as though the arts fare better than the sciences in old age: Thomas Hardy wrote fine poetry in his eighties and Picasso is still painting controversially, also in his eighties. Bernard Shaw wrote his best plays after he was forty-five but his last half-dozen are less good than his early and middle-period plays. On the other hand, the German writer, Fontane, began writing his highly successful novels in his seventies. Goethe was over eighty when he finished writing *Faust* and Titian was nearly ninety when he did some of his finest work. In mathematics and the physical sciences, however, most of the best work seems to be done by young people. This may be because science has more objective, less shifting standards of value – despite the fact that it has developed at an ever-accelerating rate. It may be also because in pure mathematics and the physical sciences, success demands essentially the finding of new interpretations or the invention of new methods.

This tallies quite well with what is known of test performances at different ages. Traditional intelligence tests, with their stress on deductive reasoning and on quick, accurate observation, rather than on familiarity with specific subject-matter, tend to be better predictors in such fields as mathematics, science and engineering. It has been mentioned that vocabulary tests are about the only cognitive tests to date in which the middle-aged and older can compete with their juniors. The capacity of playwrights and novelists to continue to practise their craft is presumably related to this.

If a generalization must be made as to the most intellectually fruitful period in life, the answer would be in the thirties.[7] The majority of successes in all fields occur during this period, despite many exceptions. This makes sense, since at this stage one is sufficiently mature to have acquired valuable experience, but sufficiently young to be scarcely past the peak period of intelligence as measured (see Fig. 1). Throughout life, however, the inseparability of intellect and temperament should not be forgotten.

We have seen that the older person tends to pick up ideas and skills more slowly, to reason less cogently and to remember less efficiently than he did when he was young. He tends also to be less flexible and less fluent – in the sense of being more perseverative[Y], less able as well as less willing to go off at a tangent. Here we are clearly straddling the artificial distinction between cognition and orexis once again. In fact, in later life their inseparability may become even more important than in early adulthood and early middle age, since at this stage self-confidence often begins to wane. The lessening in confidence is sometimes due to the individual's awareness of his decreasing powers – of concentration, of memory and of mental and physical energy: he realizes, perhaps obscurely, that 'trying a little harder' will no longer do the trick and also, perhaps, that the reserves on which he used to draw for trying harder, are drying up.

Diminishing self-confidence may be reflected either in an access of didactic loquacity and autocratic behaviour or, on the contrary, in hesitancy, indecision and placatory bowing to the pronouncements of others. Or the same person may vacillate between these two modes of compensation. In this short account some common personality factors between very old age and very early youth are discernible. We begin to see the appropriateness of the phrase 'second childhood'. There are certain characteristics, however, which seem to be possessed by the aged rather than the young, which may be advantageous. One tends to become more self-critical when older, perhaps as a result of experience: observation of oneself now, in contrast to the past, to others, or to some ideal never to be realized. Self-criticism is very clearly part cognitive and part orectic. One tends also to be slower to argue, when older.

This discussion of the cognitive-cum-orectic changes with age, brings us back to the chapter heading, 'When the age is in, the wit is out.' For 'wit' has two (closely related) meanings here, the mainly cognitive and the mainly orectic. It can mean (a) intelligence, cleverness, good sense or (b) a kind of dry linguistic humour. And sure enough, advancing age seems to reduce our wit, in both senses. As described above, intelligence – whether as 'measured' or as displayed in real life situations – tends to diminish as we grow older. In general, we also grow less witty and less humorous. We are apt to take ourselves more seriously and to lose something of our capacity both for appreciating and for producing wit. Anybody who has much to do with young people and, especially, with children will be struck by the ease and joy with which they entertain the impossible (wittingly so); their capacity for perpetrating endlessly and unapologetically the most excruciating puns and far-fetched allusions; and the extent to which they indulge in 'it would be fun if . . .' fantasy.

Wit and humour demand a capacity for detaching oneself from one aspect of the situation and, in particular, for disengaging oneself emotionally. It is *remarks* which are witty and they can be said (and appreciated) only by somebody who is not wholly involved, personally, in the topic of conversation. The classic situation of slipping on a banana skin (at the end of the humour spectrum furthest from wit) is usually seen as funny by all except the sufferer; but it sometimes is perceived as such by him – if he momentarily deserts his role as the one who slipped and takes on the role of the onlooker who sees 'how funny it must have looked'. Such an incident is an example of primitive humour – primitive both in the sense of being universal and of appealing to our baser instincts. The laugher generally contains an element of 'rather he than I' – even when the laugher and the sufferer are one and the same. Wit perhaps provokes a smile rather than a laugh: it is quieter, more astringent and more intellectual.

In any case, the wit tends to be 'out' when 'the age is in'. We laugh and we smile less as we grow older for we are less easily amused and pleased. Our rationalization may take the form of superiority – 'it is childish to laugh at *that*' – or of sophistication – 'I've heard this sort of thing so many times.' The promotion of amusement, the presentation of the incongruous as such, and the recognition of similarity, where it is common to perceive diversity only – also tends to decline with age, largely owing to our growing mental rigidity. We are increasingly apt to pursue our thoughts and doings in a straight line, as we get older (unlike de Bono's 'lateral thinker'[8]). If we look neither to right nor left, we lose the faculty of disengagement wherein lies the secret of wit.

William James has said that 'Genius in truth means little more than the faculty of perceiving in an unhabitual way.' This faculty, in most people, steadily decreases with age – as, not unnaturally, we steadily acquire more numerous and more ingrained habits.

Thus, the changes with age permeate our whole personality. Mercifully, however, ageing does not affect everybody in exactly the same way. Some exemplify the dictum: 'If a man is not a socialist when he is young, he has no heart; if he is not a tory when he is old, he has no head' (implying that we would all rather have heads than hearts) whilst others grow steadily more liberal-minded over the years. Some put increasing emphasis on 'correctness' in the sense of conformity while others become more 'live and let live' as they grow older. Some become more intense and anxious, while others grow calmer and more placid. Some mellow, but others sour with the years. Whilst many old people look nostalgically backward most of the time, some resolutely look forward, hand in hand with their grandchildren. As in the cognitive field, although certain limits are set by our physical constitution, the events in our life largely determine how we react in later life – and the way the world treats us depends largely upon ourselves.

14 The Mediocrity of Women

Vive La Différence!

Mediocrity of women – Cognitive differences between the sexes –
Differences in temperament between the sexes – Inequality
of opportunity

Five points are worthwhile making on the cognitive differences
between males and females. First, there is a tendency for men to
be 'more so' than females, whatever is being tested. Thus on
intelligence tests, for instance, when groups of comparable young
men and women take tests, they tend to gain mean scores [z]
which are similar, but the highest and the lowest scorers are
liable to be male. This finding is not confined to intelligence
tests or even to psychological tests in general. It applies also to
academic examinations.[1] There is a tendency for women students
to gain proportionately more second class degrees – and, thus,
fewer firsts and thirds – in many examination subjects. This applies even to Oxbridge where, owing to the sex ratio in the university, the competition for Oxbridge places among girls leaving
school is stiffer than it is among boys. It might therefore have been
supposed that these young women, being still more highly selected, would obtain a higher proportion of first class degrees. This
is not the case, however, and in my opinion, the reason is not simply prejudice on the part of the (predominantly male) examiners.

In the 'real world' situation, the same tendency holds: men
rather than women are found at the extremes. There are more male
geniuses, more male criminals, more male mental defectives,
suicides and stutterers, more colour blind males, than females.
The list is a long one, with relatively few exceptions. Whether
this is due primarily to the biological functions of women may
become clarified within the next half-century. In any case, the fact
that there are far more eminent men than women, past and
present, is not wholly explicable on sociological grounds – i.e.

that higher education for women is less than a hundred years old, that until recently it was not considered quite nice for a woman to have a career; and that even now a professional career for a woman is thought by many to be incompatible with, and inferior to, wifehood and motherhood.

It is true that women clergymen are not yet acceptable; that in many industries women are banned from the executive and administrative dining rooms; that women engineers are still considered an oddity (except perhaps in iron-curtain countries); and that women were still fighting for the right to be allowed to qualify medically in the late 1860s. On this point, it is worth quoting the memorable comment published in the *Lancet* in 1865 with reference to Elizabeth Garrett Anderson's defiant passing of the Society of Apothecaries' examination – the only one open to her if she wished to become a doctor. 'No doubt', said the *Lancet*, 'the examiners had due regard for her sex and omitted all those subjects of examination which would be shocking to the female mind'![2] Less entertaining is the subsequent revision of the Society of Apothecaries' constitution, specifically to exclude women from their examinations.

The supremacy of men, however, is maintained in such fields as painting, composing and sculpture – as well as in industry, engineering and medicine – i.e. in fields in which it has long been considered respectable for women to excel. Even in writing, the number of great women novelists is small; whilst the number of great women poets is minute. This is strange in view of the alleged verbal superiority of the female (see below). As for scientific research: the existence of one Marie Curie proves that social difficulties can be overcome by the rare woman who has the necessary combination of gifts and guts.[3]

Thus, despite what is said above about the relative scarcity of female geniuses (along with the relative scarcity of colour-blind women and female criminals), there are some egregious women. Indeed these tend to be considered all the more outstanding on account of their rarity. Women murderers often excite more disgust, and women novelists more admiration, than their male counterparts. In some fields, such as medicine, dentistry and veterinary science, women actually have to be better than men in order to obtain the opportunity for training.

The second male/female difference takes us back to the statement (page 136) that 'they tend to gain mean scores which are similar'. This applies to intelligence test results in general but sex differences do obtain with respect to the preferred bias in a test. Broadly speaking, females do relatively better in verbally biased items and males do better in numerical and diagrammatic items – and also in mechanical problems, in the sense of problems requiring an understanding of mechanical principles. This too, strong feminists and men generously 'leaning over backwards', have sought to explain on sociological grounds ('little boys are given model aircraft and cars and meccano, whereas little girls are given dolls, crayons and soft materials to play with'). But strong-minded girls have a way of borrowing their brothers' toys. Furthermore, these facts concerning mechanical ability tie up with the findings on diagrammatic and spatial problems[AA] and these in turn tie up with the science/arts question which is discussed later in this chapter.

As to the relative verbal superiority of girls: it has long been observed that baby girls tend to speak earlier, and to speak more, than baby boys. (It is sometimes claimed, usually by men, that this difference continues – is, indeed, exacerbated – throughout life!) Attempts to show that this is due to the infant's environment – that the mother tends to talk more, and give more verbal encouragement to, her baby daughter than her baby son – are not wholly convincing.[4]

The question of rate of development leads on to the third point for discussion. The headmasters of co-educational junior schools find that the girls tend to develop earlier, intellectually, than the boys. (This is true also of their physical and emotional development.) Thus if 11 + results were taken at their face value, more girls than boys would be gaining grammar school places (in those areas where grammar school selection still takes place). A year or two later, however, the boys put on their intellectual spurt and come into their own academically. It is therefore considered best to make allowance for this difference and deliberately to allocate equal numbers of male and female places at eleven. Indeed, once puberty is reached, boys tend to catch up with or surpass girls even on verbally biased problems. From adolescence on, the 'female relative superiority' mentioned above requires a stress on the word 'relative'.

The fourth point concerns creativity and refers to adults rather than children. It has been suggested that artists and creative people generally, tend towards greater cross-sex identification than do the rest of us, i.e. that they have somewhat greater bi-sexual tendencies.[5] Most would agree that sexuality lies on a continuum, as opposed to the rigid dichotomy which used to be assumed: that most men possess some degree of femininity and that most women possess some degree of masculinity. This is confirmed both by the results on psychometric scales of masculinity/femininity[6] and also by reflective observation outside the psychological laboratory. The hypothesis, then, is that the creative man – in whatever field – tends to have more femininity in his psychological makeup than has the less creative man, and that the creative woman tends to possess more masculine traits than does the less creative woman. This is difficult to prove or refute since some element of semantic circularity seems inevitable but it is an interesting and thought-provoking suggestion.

Fifth are the male/female differences which align themselves to a considerable degree with some science/arts differences. The recipe for achievement in science might read: 'Take a handful of facts (not previously associated with one another); fold in one or two original, highly specific ideas; allow time to mature; make strictly relevant deductions; flavour with piquant generalizations.' The chef would be typically male. On the other hand, the recipe for achievement in the arts might read: 'First catch your idea; allow it to free-associate in a congenial atmosphere; immerse the resultant mixture in rose-coloured sauce (if for nineteenth century consumption) or in midnight-blue pickles (if for twentieth century consumption); let it rise if it will.' The chef will again tend to be male but there are more female competitors – and the number is growing.

The male-science/female-arts difference may, in all seriousness, be a congenital difference rather than a social artefact, but it is hard to tell as long as society continues to treat women as intellectually different from men. It is very similar to the question of colour prejudice: only a minority candidly admit to it but the majority of whites (and of men) behave in accordance with the prejudice and it is the whites (and the males) who have the upper hand, i.e. who largely determine the conventions followed and the line toed by all but a few dissidents and eccentrics.

If this be considered an exaggeration, consider the following statement, drawn from a recent book by a psychiatrist who has spent his working life studying human beings and their relationships.[7]

The hypothesis that women, if only given the opportunity and encouragement, would equal or surpass the creative achievements of men is hardly defensible . . . No doubt it is important that men should reach the stars, or paint the Sistine Chapel or compose nine symphonies. But it is equally vital that we should be cherished and fed, and that we should reproduce ourselves. Women have no need to compete with men; for what they alone can do is the more essential.

The writer goes on to describe 'the creative activities of childbearing and the making of a home' (as though these are incompatible with less earthy creative activities) but, later on in the book, he writes of '*the dreadful fact* that, every year, the world has 63 million new mouths to feed' (my italics). This presents a striking combination of complacent (though kindly) male reassurance and unwitting (still male) inconsistency.

This discussion of men and women in the cognitive field may be summed up as follows. First, the top rungs of the achievement ladder are certainly occupied by men and this is very likely a basic psychological fact – as opposed to a sociological one – since the bottom rungs of this and other ladders tend also to be occupied by men. The findings of some social anthropologists are worth considering here. But, secondly, the truth of this basic psychological hypothesis cannot be determined until women have had strictly equal vocational, social and educational opportunities *for many generations*. Thirdly, so far as women are taking advantage of their slowly and hardly-won quasi-equality, their gifts appear to equip them for the arts rather than the sciences. Since this applies to girls who attended co-educational schools, it cannot be explained simply in terms of the poorer science and mathematics teaching which is sometimes said to perpetuate a vicious spiral.[8]

It was foreseeable that discussion of the cognitive aspects of sex differences should lead to discussion of differences in temperament between the sexes. We have seen that there are certain intellectual differences and that some of these may be congenital, though it is evident that these cannot be expressed simply, or in the form of sweeping generalisations. Are there any parallel differences in temperament? And, if so, we may ask again, are they due to the impact of a society run, as it is, essentially by and for men? Or is the form of our culture itself due to the psychological differences between the sexes? The answer would appear to be 'yes' to both the latter questions.

If one asks men and women what they consider to be the main psychological differences between the sexes, a considerable measure of agreement is found. Women are said to be (a) more 'personal-minded' than men; (b) to be less interested in abstract matters; (c) to be more prone to have, and to back, hunches; (d) to be more conscientious over small details[9]; (e) to have more scruples; (f) to be less interested than men in political, economic and military matters; (g) to be more catty. Most people of both sexes would be inclined to agree with these – with the possible exception of (g). But, expanded, the wording might become recognizably distinct for the two sexes. It will be clear to members of both sexes which point of view is given first, below.

(a) may be interpreted as (i) 'genuinely interested in other people' or as (ii) 'always harping on personalities'. (b), rather closely related, may be expressed (i) as 'interested in practical realities rather than in theorizing' or (ii) as 'having no interest in ideas as such'. (c) (i) 'Women have and use more intuition than men.' (ii) 'Women's judgements are emotional and not based on any rational grounds.' (d) (i) 'It's the small things in life that matter.' (ii) 'Women can't see the wood for the trees.' (e) (i) 'Men are often ruthless.' (ii) 'Any action here is better than none.'

(*f*) does not need to be rewritten: it is acceptable to both sexes, as it stands. (*g*), not surprisingly, is more acceptable to men than to women, however expressed. In the writer's opinion, however, it contains some truth and it is likely to be due partly to women's greater interest in matters personal, partly to their reluctance to use physical force and partly to the fact that, as shown below, women still have less opportunity of intellectual fulfilment than do men.

(*g*) is closely linked with (*a*), (*b*) and (*d*). Indeed the seven points intermingle and link with one another to such an extent that it is not practicable to discuss them separately. Perhaps the best way to appraise them is to consider a few jobs which, by common consent, are performed better in general by women than by men. For this purpose we must include occupations of varied socio-economic levels.

Women seem to make especially good industrial inspectors (recognizing tiny flaws), personal secretaries, teachers of young children, social workers, nurses and telephone operators. (Question: why are there so few female radio and television announcers? Answer: Because men consider that women tend to come over 'too personally'). Air hostesses are famed for their efficiency and charm. It is immediately apparent that, with the exception of the industrial inspecting, all these occupations require an interest in and a liking for people. The jobs demand patience and sympathy with others who may not be at their best (this applies to nurses and social workers, particularly, and occasionally to personal secretaries) and who may be ingeniously infuriating for long periods (this applies especially to teachers of young children). If people holding these jobs should have to cope with political, economic or business matters, it is incidentally only. All are dealing with concrete rather than abstract problems; all need, in their way, to pay scrupulous attention to detail.

In my opinion, this last trait is related to woman's famed (or infamous) 'intuition'. This is neither a mystical sixth sense nor is it an utterly unfounded myth. Women's so-called intuitive judgements and perceptions are due not so much to some vague, generalized sensitivity as to acute awareness of a number of small personal details – an awareness which may not even be recognized at the time. Women often have this to a greater extent than men because they are more interested in the small personal details – a change in facial expression, a hesitation in replying, an unusual intonation, a minor alteration in the arrangement of a room. They are interested in the details for their own sake and also for what they signify. Since they are sometimes unwilling to disclose these sources of their opinions, and sometimes unable to do so – and since the interpretations based on these niceties are sometimes correct – the result is often labelled 'intuition'. The word may be pronounced contemptuously or smugly, according to choice.

Women's alleged cattiness, again, is largely due to their being more interested than men in the small personal pettinesses which constitute the subject-matter of cattiness. The word connotes littleness, pettiness and the figurative use of claws, i.e. spiteful utterances. There is little doubt that women *mind* more than men about day-to-day personal matters. On the other hand, they have recourse to physical reprisal less readily than do men. They therefore use their traditional weapon – words – and 'cattiness' is the result.

Let us end by discussing an activity which is pursued by both sexes and which roughly half of the adult population (the male half) believes to be carried out far better by men than by women: driving a car. Everybody in our culture is familiar with this activity, whether as a passenger, a driver or a pedestrian. Is the standard joke about women drivers well founded? Or is it based on the quicksands of prejudice? Impartial observation of driving in all conditions suggests that the typical faults of a woman driver are neither graver nor milder than the typical faults of a man driver. But they are *different* faults. The below-average woman driver is apt to shilly-shally, to hesitate, to slow down – without actually stopping or drawing right in to the nearside; she tends to drive more slowly than her husband, to drive too near to the centre of the road, to get into the wrong stream through not knowing her way and to take too long to make up her mind one way or the other, about overtaking. Thus she may innocently goad the male driver behind her into a piece of dangerous driving, though she will probably not actively sin in this respect herself.

Her male counterpart tends to jump the queue at a roundabout or in a procession of cars crawling along behind a lorry; he is apt to push by and then have to cut in; he often drives faster than conditions of safety allow; he is more likely to drive as though in a perpetual hurry and – however long he has been driving – he continues to expect others on the road to behave sensibly and politely. His own manners tend to be far worse in, than outside, a car.

These two pictures are not drawn as typical female and male drivers but as typical of poor drivers of their respective sexes. And these impressionistic pictures are confirmed by the accident figures for men and women. One of the most important insurance companies (the Zurich Group) insures women drivers at twenty per cent lower premium than men drivers. This does not imply – a spokesman of the group hastens to explain – that women drive better than men. It is based on careful statistical research: this has revealed that, mile for mile, men drivers tend to have more serious accidents than women. 'The typical woman's car-accident results in a scratched wing or a bent bumper,' says a Zurich Group insurance expert, 'her accidents tend to occur at low speed. Whereas men's accidents tend to be more damaging to the cars and the people concerned.' Mile for mile, women drivers actually have more recorded accidents than male drivers[10] but the women's accidents are, in general, far less costly.

These figures do take into account the fact that there are more male drivers than female drivers on the road and that the men tend to drive longer hours than the women. The difference in type and severity of road accidents is said by the (male) expert mentioned above, to be due to 'the more enterprising' style of driving favoured by the men, i.e. their preference for speed and for occasional risk-taking. This is said to be linked with the concept of the car as a phallic symbol.

Thus some members of both sexes can and do drive badly; the faults committed differ, predictably, as between men and women; and male drivers – who form the majority – are less tolerant of the typical female faults than they are of the typical male faults. Finally, let us consult the blueprint on pages 141–2. We have seen that in certain jobs some characteristically feminine traits may be assets. We can now see how these traits can operate as defects in certain circumstances. The faults of the woman who drives badly stem from her more personal interests, her attention to immediate details and her scruples. She havers, instead of overtaking, because she is paralysingly aware of the possibilities and the results of having an accident; she gets less kick out of taking risks; she is less keen on speed, whether as an end or a means. If she boasts, it is of her accident-free driving record; if her husband boasts, it is of the record time in which he completed his journey.

To sum up: in attainment and also in cognitive testing, the top performers tend to be male. It may be relevant that the lowest performers tend also to be male. The intellectual superiority of men may be due partly to the subjection of women: certainly the proportion of eminent women is steadily growing. This increase has occurred most swiftly during the last two generations – which is also the period during which women have won most rights. It is unlikely, however, that the sexes will approximate ever more closely in their attitudes, interests and dispositions. Indeed it would be a pity were this to happen, for it is very clear that people all along the sexual continuum have much of value to offer.

15 The Existence of Psychological Phenomena

Letting a hundred flowers blossom and a hundred schools of thought contend – MAO TSE-TUNG

*Existence of psychological phenomena in their own right –
How relevant is animal behaviour to human experience ? –
Application of ' experimental ' to subject-matter rather than
method – Widening the horizon of experimental psychology*

Two main themes run through this book. The first is that psychological phenomena exist and are worthy of study in their own right. By 'psychological phenomena' is meant such experiences as 'having toothache' (as opposed to 'dental caries') or 'seeing a red patch' (as opposed to 'the occurrence of the wavelength 0·00062 millimetres') – a couple of examples used in Chapter 13. Other examples of psychological phenomena are having dreams (not to be equated with rapid eye movements or change in EEG or having eaten cheese for supper – or even to a combination of these and other physical facts); feeling apprehensive (not to be equated with rapid breathing, raised blood pressure, sweating, increased rate of heart beat, etc., nor with our awareness of these changes – when awareness does occur – whatever James and Lange may have said[1]); solving problems, and failing to solve them; changing one's mind; admiring a picture; having a tune 'on the brain'; learning a poem by heart; enjoying a meal.

These are all psychological phenomena, in the relevant sense. Some involve observable appropriate behaviour and some do not. It is not denied that behaviour, too, should form a part of psychological study. But it *is* denied that psychology can be reduced to any form of behaviourism, naïve or sophisticated. Experimental psychologists have been attempting to do just this ever since the days of J. B. Watson.[2] Their aim is the reduction of experimental psychology to an exact science, quantifiable, analogous to physics rather than biology. In the writer's opinion this is highly unscientific since it involves the deliberate neglect of many facts of experience, the distortion of other facts to fit theories and the equating of processes which are patently not equivalent. This approach to psychology has resulted in endless series of largely sterile experiments, mostly conducted with great expertise in accordance with the most stringent methodological principles, the results being analysed often in accordance with unimpeachable statistics. Let us consider two examples of this 'experimental' approach.

Tens of thousands of rats have been run through thousands of mazes; dozens of learning theories have been propounded; and a ritualistic game is now played by the experimenters – a game whose ultimate goal seems to have been lost sight of and whose rationale is not defined (and which is far from clear to psychologists whose game is not the rat-in-maze). Meanwhile the teachers of school children and of future teachers, and the university students of psychology who are as yet unindoctrinated, ask plaintively what has been discovered by this extensive experimentation, why the proliferating theories must be learned, since their interest is historical only, and how such experiments apply – if they do – to human beings.

The educationists tend to remain recalcitrant. But the university students, after a year or two, either become brain-washed into believing that all animals are rats, that all learning situations are mazes and that all learners are manipulable by some external god-devil – or they decide that 'experimental psychology' is not for them and they go off into psychoanalysis or 'clinical' or 'educational' psychology. The quotation marks are inserted because of the implication that 'clinical' and 'educational' psychology are incompatible with an experimental approach. This viewpoint is discussed below.

The second example concerns 'linguistics' and 'communication'; again the quotation marks are necessary. Before the schism between Experimental Psychologists and The Rest occurred, psychologists used to be interested in *language* and also in communication – in the sense of intelligible contact between living beings. Now, in order to remain within the coveted experimental fold one must, sheeplike, deal with 'linguistics' – a kind of meta-language – and 'communication' – a kind of mathematical model, several places removed from the actual making of contact between individual human beings. The units tend to be digits or letters or nonsense syllables, rarely words, and practically never meaningful sentences, relevant to a real-life situation.

The original reason for abandoning meaningful material when researching on human learning or recall, was that such material has values and associations and that these will vary with the individual. Therefore, reasoned the early experimental psychologists, it is not possible to conduct controlled experiments using meaningful material. One must eliminate the meaning so that everybody can start equal. Thus was born the cult of the nonsense syllable.

Later experimenters, however, discovered that even nonsense syllables have some associations, and some syllables have more than others. This was always evident to introspective Subjects but it now has the cachet of having been experimentally demonstrated. Indeed a scale of associative value has been constructed for the most frequently used nonsense syllables. What apparently remains to be rediscovered, after Bartlett,[3] is that such experiments do not necessarily throw much light on learning and remembering in everyday life. He showed (a) that the psychological laws followed in real life situations are sometimes different from those which are followed in laboratory situations and (b) that it is possible, though difficult, to use experimental methods when tackling the problems of everyday life remembering and forgetting. Very few of his successors have followed this up.[4]

We may now return to our first theme: strictly psychological phenomena exist. Such phenomena should not be *identified with* their underlying physiological mechanisms, nor can they be satisfactorily explained by experimentation on simpler and more quantifiable material – whether such material be the memorizing of digits in different conditions, the time taken to sort cards given certain instructions, the experimental neuroses of cats or the co-operative behaviour of pigeons. Much of this work is valuable but it should be carried out in addition to careful observation, introspection and experimentation on the more complex data of non-laboratory life. Let a hundred flowers blossom!

One consequence of the obsessively behaviouristic and mechanistic approach is the apparent callousness of much of the experimental work carried out on the lower animals, often without any obvious worthwhile aim. Let us take five examples from the many which, distressingly, abound. (a) Rats have been continuously deprived of sleep for 27 consecutive days, by means of placing them in a continuously rotating wheel (2 r.p.m.), two-thirds submerged in water. 'The rats, when exhausted, fell from the wheel into the water and were unable to remount the wheel.' 'The Subjects found ways of sleeping by hanging on food trays and, in one case, climbing to the top of the cubicle and sleeping while hanging with front teeth hooked in the hardware cloth top. Modifications were introduced to prevent this.'[5] (b) Young puppies have been separated from their mothers and litter-mates, reared in small bare cages in extreme isolation, fed by a mechanism which ensures that they have no contact with any living being and kept on a 'harsh and irregular' diet. (c) Male rats have been forced 'into making sexual approaches to another male rat – mounting and pelvic thrusts, etc. – by keeping them on an electric grid and shocking them through the feet, then turning the shock off whenever they commenced the homosexual behaviour'. (d) Monkeys have had (notoriously agonizing) 'executive ulcers' induced. (e) Monkeys and other animals have been made 'experimentally addicted' to alcohol, morphine and other drugs and then allowed to suffer the well-known withdrawal effects.[6]

It is sometimes stated in defence of such experiments that they cannot be performed on man. Comparable work with human beings is, admittedly, difficult. It involves, for instance, the finding of suitable Subjects and controls, instead of having them readily available in the laboratory. It requires, too, the establishing of rapport with the Subjects and, sometimes, with their doctors, instead of manipulating animals who have no option. But the existence of ready-made human drug- and alcohol-addicts is very evident – as is that of humans with ulcers, whether 'executive' or otherwise. In fact, this problem was investigated in a well-controlled experiment by the Industrial Health Research Board as early as 1937.[7] Again, the willingness of some men and women to forego sleep voluntarily for many consecutive days was amply demonstrated in the late 1920s when tests of endurance, thinly disguised as 'dancing competitions', were well supported.* The validity of extrapolating from volunteers to non-volunteers may be dubious but it is surely no more so than is extrapolating from the behaviour of rats or cats to the behaviour of mankind. Moreover humans can offer introspection – to those psychologists who accept this as potentially useful – whilst the lower animals cannot.

The work on 'animal behaviour' is always expressed in scientific, hygienic-sounding terminology, which enables the indoctrination of the normal, non-sadistic young psychology student to proceed without his anxiety being aroused. Thus, techniques of 'extinction' are used for what is in fact torturing by thirst or near-starvation or electric-shocking; 'partial reinforcement' is the term for frustrating an animal by only occasionally fulfilling the expectations which the experimenter has aroused in the animal by previous training; 'negative stimulus' is the term used for subjecting an animal to a stimulus which he avoids, if possible. The term 'avoidance' is O.K. because it is an observable activity. The terms 'painful' or 'frightening stimulus' are less O.K. since they are anthropomorphic [BB]; they imply that the animal has feelings – and that these may be similar to human feelings. This is not allowable because it is non-behaviouristic and unscientific (and also because this might deter the younger and less hard-boiled researcher from pursuing certain ingenious experiments. He might allow a little play to his imagination.) The cardinal sin for the experimental psychologist working in the field of 'animal behaviour' is anthropomorphism. Yet if he did not believe in the analogue of the human being and the lower animals, even he, presumably, would find his work largely unjustified. He is indeed somewhat dissociated at present, since he believes in the analogue both of humans and animals and in that of humans and

*Photographs of these were shown in the flashbacks of the 1968 film based on the life of Gertrude Lawrence, entitled *Star*.

machines. The reply of a (Nobel-prize winning) biological scientist to the question 'Do you believe that a machine can experience pain?' was 'It depends what you mean by "experience pain".'

That the experimentalist's judgement, sensibility and common sense are undermined by the uncritical acceptance of the behaviouristic attitude is well illustrated by the following extract from *The Science of Animal Behaviour*. These lines are by an English writer regarded, on both sides of the Atlantic, as an authority in experimental psychology.[6]

It is not possible to consider behaviour shown by an animal in a threatening situation as abnormal – that is, when the animal does something apparently stupid which does not solve the situation for it – without presupposing powers of deduction that the animal almost certainly does not possess. That is to say, if the animals had been allowed to do so they might have starved rather than face the shock or threat of it. Yet we cannot regard this as biologically abnormal, unless we assume the animal really knew that the shock itself was not potentially fatal, that the experimenter was not, in fact, trying to kill it.

So much for the submission that psychological phenomena exist, and are worthy of study, in their own right. The second main theme of this book is the deprecation of schisms and dichotomies in psychology – and in particular the traditional dichotomy of 'intelligence' and 'personality' as tested. The way in which the phrase 'experimental psychology' has come to be used ever widens the gulf between the 'experimental pyschologists' (or the behavioural scientists or the mechanists) on the one hand, and the clinical, social, educational, humanistic psychologists, on the other. 'Experimental psychology' has come to denote primarily certain subject-matters – such as the physiology of the central nervous system and the special senses, information theory, the rat-in-maze – just as much as it denotes the development and application of experimental method. Yet experimental method can and should be used by clinicians, educationists, etc. in their research; and when they do so their work should be of interest to the 'experimental psychologist'. It tends, however, to be ignored by him.

Psychology is not a proper realm for the promotion of dichotomies. Discrete variables are the exception rather than the rule. We have seen that masculinity-femininity forms a continuum. This is equally true of mental illness and mental health. These lie on a continuum which may be represented as a circle. The points on the circumference differ from one another in degree when close together, but in kind when they are sufficiently far apart.

FIGURE 2

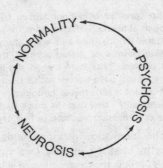

Figure 2 gives a more accurate picture of the viewpoint of most psychiatrists than does a rigid distinction between the three pairs: normality/neurosis, normality/psychosis, neurosis/psychosis. This point of view is important whether one is concerned primarily with diagnosis, with treatment or with research. The sharp divisions may appear attractively clear and suggestive of progress – just as the choice of simplified subject-matter discussed above may appear attractively objective and scientific – but ultimately it is seen to obscure rather than to clarify.

The dichotomy between 'intelligence' as tested and 'personality' as tested is misleading for three reasons. First, it involves the use of two everyday words, the technical psychological sense of 'intelligence' being far closer to the meaning given it by the layman (despite his occasional protests) than is the technical sense of 'personality'. Intelligence tests have been validated largely in accordance with commonsense assumptions but personality tests have hardly been validated at all.[8] (They have been operationally defined and validated. This allows of a shifting of position every so often.)

Secondly, insofar as personality tests do assess aspects of temperament and character, the aspects chosen are arbitrary and variable. Thirdly, and most important, the use of 'personality tests' to mean 'tests of temperament and character' obscures the close relationship between the cognitive and the orectic aspects of the living being. It suggests that they are separate, and separately measurable. This has been psychometrically convenient but it is psychologically false.

We have suggested in this book that it is desirable to design more broadly-based tests, which allow both aspects of *the total personality* to be displayed; and that this can perhaps be done by devising open-ended tests, which have objectively correct (and, of course, incorrect) answers and which differ, again objectively, in their degree of correctness. It is claimed that the open-endedness renders the tests more interesting to the Subject, less trivial, more like real-life problems and also that it allows scope for the scoring of certain orectic traits in addition to cognitive traits.

It is not suggested that this is the *only* way to devise psychometric tests, nor that the experimental psychologist should study human experience exclusively. What is suggested is a widening of the experimental psychologist's horizon to include these as well as the accepted, long-pursued disciplines of physiological psychology, cybernetics, animal behaviour, ergonomics and traditional psychometrics. It is true that the underlying physiological mechanisms are highly relevant and that they need to be understood if psychological theories are not to run riot; that cybernetic analogies are stimulating, whether mathematical, electronic, chemical or mechanical; that studies of animal behaviour – especially those of the ethologists [CC] – are interesting in their own right and have sometimes proved instructive with respect to human behaviour; and that psychometrics has produced a considerable body of data that is useful in practice.

If the experimentalists could appreciate the blindness which results from closing their eyes to the fact of experience, and the non-experimentalists would accept the importance of carefully designed research and strictly controlled experiments: if the two factions could drop their mutual contempt and find some common ground from which to co-operate: then psychology might convincingly become a science – and a science taking forward strides, rather than trudging round in small circles. The plea is for greater imagination, both intellectual and emotional, in order that more flowers should blossom, fewer weeds should flourish and more schools of thought should contend.

Notes

A. operationism (pp. 17 and 45)

'When I use a word, it means just what I choose it to mean –
neither more nor less. . . . The question is which is to be master –
that's all.' Lewis Carroll

Through The Looking Glass

Hilgard* writes that

psychologists have widely accepted a principle called *operationism*.
Operationism is not itself a system of psychology; it is a principle according to which scientific statements keep their reference to data from
experiments. The term comes from Bridgman,† a physicist, who said
that we know physical concepts only according to the *operations* by
which we arrive at them. Thus we specify temperature according to the
readings of the height of a mercury column in a dry-bulb thermometer,
calibrated in certain ways in accordance with the freezing and boiling
points of water ... A sensory threshold is defined by the psycho-
physical method used in deriving it, for that method defines the operations needed to verify the result.

Similarly Brodbeck‡ (quoted by Butcher, 1968) says that

the characteristic abstractness of scientific concepts, like mass or IQ,
lies in the fact that these terms cannot be defined by simply listing a
cluster of directly observable attributes. Merely by looking at a surface
we can tell whether it is red or by looking at an object whether it is a
gnu. [*Both these examples seem debatable to the present writer.*] We
cannot so simply tell what the mass of an object or the IQ of a child is.

*Hilgard, E. R., *Introduction to Psychology*, Harcourt Brace, New York,
1953.

†Bridgman, P. W., *The Logic of Modern Physics*, Macmillan, New York,
1927.

‡Brodbeck, M., 'Logic and scientific method in research on teaching',
Chapter 2 in Gage, N. L., (Ed.), *Handbook of Research on Teaching*, Rand
McNally, Chicago, 1963.

Notes

These extracts have been quoted at some length in order to illustrate three points. (*a*) Operationism comes originally from the physical – not the biological – sciences. (*b*) It is legitimate to define operationally such concepts as 'temperature' since the *meaning* of the term was agreed upon before the mercury column *method* was adopted. (*c*) There are degrees of such legitimacy. Thus an operational definition of temperature or mass is wholly acceptable. Such a definition of sensory threshold is only slightly less acceptable since psychologists are agreed that the sensory threshold refers to the transitional point or zone at which a sensory stimulus becomes (or ceases to be) just perceptible – and the position of this point or zone is generally agreed to depend in part on the method used in determining it.

When, however, we consider such concepts as 'intelligence' or 'extraversion/introversion', the legitimacy of the operational definition is more questionable since the meaning of these terms is far from clear and is certainly not agreed upon. For a psychologist to insist on an operational definition here is often to build in his own infallibility: 'I hereby state that I mean by trait T that which is measured by my test of T.' If the operational psychometrist left it at that, his statement would be harmless and circular and parochial. But when he goes on to equate the T score with intelligence or introversion or creativity – without quotation marks – he is implicitly abandoning his operational position and, often, creating confusion.

B. *frequency distribution* (*pp. 17, 102 and 104*)

The frequency distribution of a test is the number of times (i.e. the frequency) with which the various possible scores on a test are gained. This can be shown either by means of (*a*) a tabulated list of the scores gained or (*b*) a histogram or (*c*) a frequency curve. Let us consider a simple example of a test, X, which has a theoretical maximum score of 20. A hundred imaginary Subjects have taken this test, none scoring over 18 or under 4. The frequency distribution of test X is shown in Figure 3, in three possible forms.

FIGURE 3

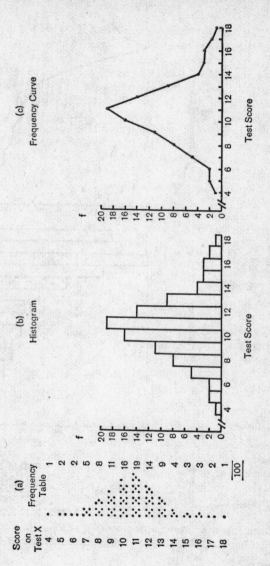

Score on Test X	(a) Frequency Table
4	1
5	2
6	2
7	5
8	8
9	11
10	16
11	19
12	14
13	9
14	4
15	3
16	3
17	2
18	1
	$\overline{100}$

(b) Histogram

(c) Frequency Curve

157

158

FIGURE 4

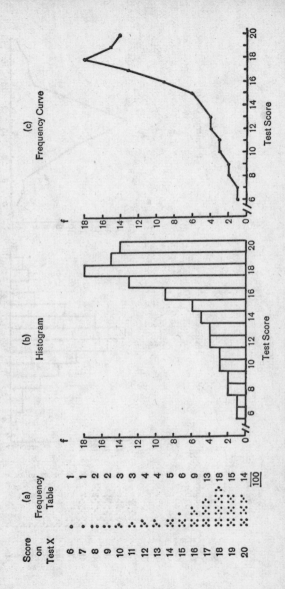

Score on Test X	(a) Frequency Table
6	1
7	1
8	2
9	2
10	3
11	3
12	4
13	4
14	5
15	6
16	9
17	13
18	18
19	15
20	14
	100

(b) Histogram

(c) Frequency Curve

FIGURE 5

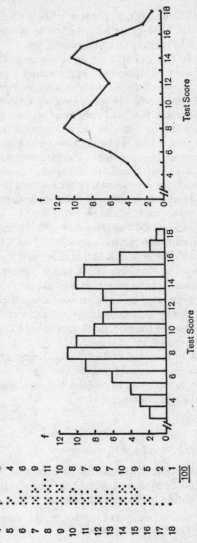

Score on Test X	Frequency Table
3	2
4	3
5	4
6	6
7	9
8	11
9	10
10	8
11	7
12	6
13	7
14	10
15	9
16	5
17	2
18	1
	100

(a)

(b) Histogram

(c) Frequency Curve

In Figure 3 (a), each dot represents a Subject's score and the shape made by the distribution of these dots is repeated in the shape of the histogram (b) and the curve (c).

In this example we have constructed a near-symmetrical frequency distribution, approaching 'normality'. That is, the majority of the Subjects gain an average score (of 10–12); fewer obtain scores slightly above and slightly below average; and extremely few gain very high or very low scores. This 'normal distribution', as the term suggests, is usual in measures of physique such as height and weight and occurs far more often than not in psychological 'measurement'.

Other types are not unknown, however. Some frequency distributions are skewed, either towards the top end of the scale or towards the lower end. See Figure 4, based on Test X and 100 other hypothetical Subjects.

In Figure 4 the frequency distribution is skewed towards the top end. The results suggest that Test X is too easy for this group of 100 Subjects: it is failing to effect differentiation at the top end, owing to bunching of the better Subjects. An artificial ceiling is imposed on them so that they are not 'extended'. If, however, X is to be used in order to spot a small proportion of very weak Subjects – in need, perhaps, of extra coaching – such a distribution curve may be more appropriate than a symmetrical distribution.

A further type of distribution referred to in the text is bi-modal – having two peaks. (*see* Figure 5.)

A full account of frequency distribution may be found in Yule and Kendall's book.*

C. criterion (*p. 17*)

A criterion is a standard or yard-stick which can be used for purposes of comparison. The most frequently used criteria for validating psychological tests are (*a*) intra-test, i.e. limited to the

*Yule, G., Udny, and Kendall, M. G., *An Introduction to the Theory of Statistics*, Chas. Griffin, 1946.

particular test to be validated, (*b*) inter-test, i.e. the criterion is some test *other than* the test in question, (*c*) factor analysis, i.e. the statistical manipulation of the scores gained on the crucial test and a number of other tests (*see* Note J).

It will be seen that all these are 'internal' criteria, in the sense that they comprise artificial, laboratory-centred measures. In the writer's view, such comparisons constitute, for the most part, evidence for *consistency* (or reliability) of various kinds, rather than for validation. The writer believes that validation demands external (i.e. non-laboratory) criteria. Mischel* (I) writes that the 'distinction between reliability and validity is not very sharp' and that 'correlations among more dissimilar tests . . . are interpreted as validity data' (*see* Note I).

The procedures Mischel refers to may be common practice but they seem to the present writer to be less than satisfactory. Indeed, Mischel says later, when discussing tests of honesty and moral behaviour:

Their answers in these hypothetical delay of reward situations were found to relate to other questionnaires dealing with trust and a variety of verbally expressed attitudes. What they said, however, *was unrelated to their actual delay of reward choices in real situations* (present writer's italics).

Such a situation is very frequently found with orectic tests and only slightly less frequently with cognitive tests. The convention has grown up that the correlation of internal, laboratory criteria with one another shall be regarded first as necessary (this is fair enough), but later as sufficient to ensure test validity. The perusal of many test manuals reveals the prevalence of this notion. The barrage of technical terms – 'construct validity', 'predictive validity', 'blurring of distinction between "validity" and "reliability"' and the like – does not succeed in its mission of concealing the sad paucity of the validation data.

*Mischel, W., *Personality and Assessment*, Wiley, 1968.

D. behaviourist (p. 18)

The term 'behaviourism' was first coined to signify a reaction against the heavy reliance on the introspective method which many psychologists were happy to accept, in the late nineteenth and early twentieth centuries. These behaviouristic psychologists said, with justice, that a few introspections did not constitute scientific evidence – particularly since the Subjects concerned were often deeply involved in the question at issue, frequently knew what introspections would be most appropriate and indeed often combined the role of theorizer and experimenter with that of introspecting Subject. Thus 'trained' Subjects were apt to be biased, but the introspections of untrained Subjects were considered by many psychologists to be unreliable. Introspection of all kinds, however, was extensively used.

The early behaviourists, as so often happens in such cases, went to the other extreme. They said that nothing should be accepted as evidence that was not observable and measurable. From this, it was a short step to infer that what is *not* observable and measurable does not exist. Thus, thought was equated with speech or incipient speech; emotion with sweating, increased adrenalin in the blood, etc.; and learning was equated with conditioning. By 'conditioning' is meant the linking of a response (such as salivating) to a new stimulus (such as the sound of a bell), as opposed to the original stimulus (in this case, food). Moreover claims were made that the human being – complete with his abilities, feelings and ambitions – could be explained if sufficient attention were paid to his conditioning from birth onwards. It was even maintained by the more extreme behaviourists that they could turn any human infant into any given type of adult, capable of succeeding in *any* occupation, if given a free hand from birth.

Experimental psychology has never really recovered from that extreme phase. It is common to find experimentalists smiling at what they call 'the naïve behaviourism of Watson' but it is far from easy to detect important differences (except in terminology) between that early behaviourism and the present-day approach.

Of course the experimental psychologist should observe behaviour and, where feasible, quantify it – outside and inside the laboratory. But it seems clear that an introspective approach needs to be combined with a behaviouristic approach, if experimental psychology is to advance the understanding of human beings.

E. heredity and environment (p. 20)

See for instance, Eysenck, H. J., *Know Your Own I.Q.*, Pelican, 1962.

It appears that about 80 per cent of all the factors contributing to individual differences of intelligence are hereditary, 20 per cent environmental; in other words, heredity is four times as important as environment.

Hebb* states (re 80 per cent heredity, 20 per cent environment) that

this statement is, on the face of it, nonsense.... To ask how much heredity contributes to intelligence is like asking, how much the width of a field contributes to its area.

F. 'innateness' of intelligence (p. 24)

Sir Cyril Burt has sometimes claimed, in recent years, that he accepts the existence of (inconstant) interaction between nature and nurture, with respect to intelligence. Indeed, in a number of passages he does pay lip-service to this. But his basic belief in the innateness of intelligence – both as measured, and as manifested outside the psychological laboratory – is clear from (a) his continued inclusion of the word 'innate' in his longstanding, and recent, *definition* of intelligence† and (b) in the following passages

*Hebb, D. O., *A Text book of Psychology*, W. B. Saunders, Co., Philadelphia & London, 1958, pp. 128–9.

†Burt, C., 'The genetic determination of differences in intelligence', *Brit. J. Psychol.*, 57, 1966, 137–53.

written, respectively, in 1937 and in 1953, typical of much of his writing.

This general intellectual factor, central and all-pervading, shows a further characteristic, also disclosed by testing and statistics. It appears to be inherited, or at least inborn. Neither knowledge nor practice, neither interest nor industry will avail to increase it. *

If, however, psychologists have agreed to use the word 'intelligence' as a convenient name for an *inborn* component of behaviour, then it becomes nonsensical to contend that by adding knowledge or skill, or by broadening the child's experience, this inborn component can itself be changed.†

To redress the balance: an interesting, and strongly environmentalist view of intelligence can be found in J. McV. Hunt's book on *Intelligence and Experience*.‡

An extreme environmentalist – viewpoint may be found in an appropriately entitled paper by Bortelmann.§ He writes that: 'The patterns of behaviour comprising intelligence are accumulative, acquired, maintained and elaborated by sequential learning experiences.'

G. multiple-choice/open-ended (pp. 29 and 37)

A multiple-choice item in a test (or examination) is one in which the problem is followed by several solutions, one and only one of which is intended to be correct. Thus, for instance, '*seldom rarely* ... SAME/OPPOSITE' is in multiple-choice form. Such items, where the choice is between two solutions only, are still fairly common (especially in tests of temperament and character) but they are open to the objection that there is a fifty per cent proba-

*Burt, C., *The Backward Child*, University of London Press, 1937.

†Burt, C., *The Causes and Treatment of Backwardness*, University of London Press, 1953.

‡Hunt, J. McV., *Intelligence and Experience*, Ronald Press, 1961.

§ Bortelmann, I. J. 'The culturally disadvantaged and compensatory education: fantasies and realities,' *News Letter No. 9 of the Assoc. of Educ. Psychologists*, 1967.

bility of choosing the correct (or the socially desirable) answer by chance, thus necessitating a far larger number of questions than is required if the number of choices per item be increased, say, to five or six. If the question be put in the form: '*seldom* means the SAME as . . . *sometimes, never, always, rarely, occasionally, often*' there is only a one in six probability of guessing the correct answer.

The advantage of multiple-choice items is that they reduce the handicap of the slow writer, since they require no writing other than one digit or letter or underlining per question, and their scoring is swift and wholly objective. They need very careful devising, however, if they are to be cogent. 'Open-ended' or 'creative answer' items include every type of test in which the Subject produces his own response, from the one-word answer to the essay. These offer greater scope to the Subject and more information to the tester. As the required answer gains in length, however, so the difficulties of the slow writer increase, as does the part played by subjectivity, and the time taken, in the scoring.

H. manipulation of group-members (p. 36)

Psychologists have, over the years, tended more and more to adopt the attitude (characteristic traditionally of politicians, rather than scientists) that the end justifies the means. This philosophy should always be viewed with suspicion, partly because ends turn out so often to be mere trends, and partly because when this principle is invoked the means, more often than not, are unappetising and they are liable, moreover, to taint the ends.

The particular case of ends-justifying-means to be considered here is the manipulation of Subjects by the experimenter, in an attempt to hasten the solving of his problem. Let us take two illustrations from the many that abound in the field of psychometrics. The first concerns the testing of 'level of aspiration' and the second is designated by its users, with unwitting irony, as a 'morality test'.

By 'level of aspiration' is meant the tendency of people to raise or lower their own standards in a particular task in accordance with their perception of their previous degree of success at the task. The dictum that nothing succeeds like success is related to both the subjective attitude and the objective performance denoted by the phrase 'level of aspiration'. Four examples are offered here to give some idea of the frequency with which the tester unashamedly manipulates his Subjects. All are quoted in the chapter on Level of Aspiration in the book edited by McV. Hunt on *Personality and the Behavior Disorders*.

(*a*) 'Chapman and Volkmann* made the first attack on this problem. By giving groups of college students comparison scores of (i) literary critics, (ii) students, (iii) WPA workers, for a test of "literary ability", they *were able to manipulate* the level of aspiration in a clearcut way. The comparison scores *were actually all equal but this fact was not known to the Subjects*.'

(*b*) 'The latter investigator [Festinger]† used as the chief experimental measure the change in goal discrepancy score from a condition in which the Subject had no scores but his own previous ones with which to compare his present performance, to an experimental condition *in which his score was made to appear either above or below* one of these groups.'

(*c*) 'The scores attributed to the group were arranged so that the individual's performance was equal, on the average, to the performance of the group. The positive or negative sign of the group goal discrepancy, however, *was reported as opposite to that of the Subject*.'

(*d*) 'Heathers‡ varied three factors of the objective situation to determine their influence on the degree of generality: the scale or units in which the performance scores were presented to the Subject, the shape of the curve which the series of performance scores followed, and the motivation of the Subjects. *Pre-arranged performance scores were used* and the Subject was asked to tell

*Chapman, D. W., and Volkmann, J., 'A social determinant of the level of aspiration,' *J. abnorm. soc. Psychol.*, 34, 1939, 225–38.

†Festinger, L., 'Wish, expectation, and group standards as factors influencing level of aspiration', *J. abnorm. soc. Psychol.*, 37, 1942. 184–200,

‡Heathers, L. B., 'Factors producing generality in the level of aspiration', *J. exper. Psychol.*, 30, 1942. 392–406,

what score he was "going to try to make on the next trial", or what his goal was.'

The 'morality test' (Getzels and Jackson)* 'consists of twenty-five problem situations, each followed by four alternative courses of action. For each situation the Subject is to choose the course of action that, in his opinion, would be best on the part of the person faced with the choice. ... In order to make the moral alternatives less attractive, *the Subjects were told* that the test had been administered to "500 typical high school students" and the frequency of their choice was given beside each alternative. The largest of *these fictitious frequencies* rarely appeared beside the "correct" response. The Subject's score was the number of times he chose the most moral alternative.'

The italics, throughout, are the present writer's. These excerpts are chosen in order to illustrate the willingness of some psychologists to mislead their Subjects and to manipulate them as puppets and also to illustrate the way in which psychologists are often, psychologically, ingenuous rather than ingenious. It seems likely that the use of such unavailing short cuts explains the extent of the discrepancies and of the stagnation which has for so long afflicted personality theory and personality assessment.

I. correlation (pp. 36, 67 and 108)

A correlation coefficient is a statistic which indicates the extent to which two variables vary concomitantly and is shown by the symbol r. Let us take, for example, two sets of scores gained on tests X and Y by the same group of Subjects. We wish to know whether (a) there is a tendency for people who score highly on test X to score highly also on test Y and for people who score poorly on test X to score poorly on test Y, or (b) the tendency is for people who score highly on test X to score *poorly* on test Y and conversely or (c) there is no association between tests X and Y: they are entirely unrelated. (There are, of course, other

*Getzels, J. W. and Jackson, P. W., *Creativity and Intelligence*, Wiley, New York, 1962, Chapter 4.

possibilities, such as that high scorers on X tend also to score highly on Y but that no relationship obtains among the average and lower scorers. This tends to happen between, for instance, tests of spatial perception and tests of intelligence. But, in order not to complicate the issue, we shall consider here only associations of types a, b and c.)

In type (a) the correlation is positive and its theoretical range is from 0 to $1 \cdot 0$. In type (b) the correlation is negative, ranging from 0 to $-1 \cdot 0$. In type (c) the correlation approximates to 0. The more closely the two sets of test scores agree with each other, the more closely the correlation coefficient approaches unity. Complete agreement between them would yield a correlation of 1. (A correlation coefficient cannot exceed unity.) In practice, a correlation of 1 does not occur.

It is important to know the statistical significance of a correlation, i.e. the frequency with which the association found between the two variables could be expected to occur as a matter of chance. Significance is shown by a value of p, which may be found by referring to appropriate tables, and shows the *probability* of an observed value of r occurring by chance. Usually a value of r which would occur by chance only once in 20 times, for which $p = 0.05$, is taken as just significant. In practical work a greater degree of significance, for example $p = 0.01$, is often desirable.

The statistical significance of a correlation varies with the number of Subjects in the group. The larger the group, the greater the degree of statistical significance attained by any given correlation. Thus, a correlation of $0 \cdot 34$, for instance, would not be significant for a group of 30 Subjects but would be significant at the 5 per cent level ($p = 0 \cdot 05$) for 40 Subjects and at the 1 per cent level ($p = 0 \cdot 01$) for 60 Subjects. Since p stands for the probability of such an association's occurring by chance, it is clear that the lower the p, the more highly significant is the result.

The (b) type of correlation, as already stated, is negative. What is said about significance in the immediately preceding paragraph applies also to negative correlations. The (c) type of correlation – that which indicates no relationship between the two variables – approaches 0.

Care must be taken in interpreting significant correlations. They rarely imply causation though this is quite often assumed. X and Y may correlate for a variety of reasons. They may, for instance, both be related to a third variable, Z; or they may be two aspects of the same (perhaps unrecognized) variable. In the rare cases where the existence of a causal connexion may be inferred it is not always easy to know whether x causes y or y causes x.

The original form of (product-moment) correlation (shown by the coefficient r) which makes use of the actual scores in the two tests, assumes that both sets of scores have a normal distribution. When this condition is not fulfilled, however, it is still possible to use one of the techniques of rank correlation – in which case the positions of the Subjects relative to one another are used instead of their scores – without necessarily assuming that the intervals between the ranks are equal. Two forms of rank correlation are in general use, the coefficients being symbolized by ρ (rho) and τ (tau), respectively.

J. factor analysis (pp. 36, 45 and 120)

'Factor analysis consists of computation and manipulation of matrices of correlation coefficients.' This sentence is drawn from an earlier book by the present writer.* It is part of a chapter which is a critique of factor analysis and its use in psychometrics. The purpose of such computation is to 'extract factors' which are then said to 'saturate', to a stated degree, one or more of the tests on which the matrix of inter-correlations was calculated.

A 'matrix', in this sense, is the table of correlation coefficients systematically set down. Thus if a battery of eight tests be used, A, B, C, D, E, F, G and H, the matrix would consist of a table in which A's correlations are shown with B, C, D, E, F, G and H: B's correlations with the remaining six tests are shown: C's correlations with the remaining five, and so on.

For a lucid account of the principles and practice of factor

*Heim, A. W., *The Appraisal of Intelligence*, Methuen, 1954. New edn 1970, N.F.E.R.

analysis in psychometry see the writings of Burt* or P. E. Vernon.†
It is essentially a means of *classifying* and it has been employed in
fields other than psychology, such as in agriculture, botany and
economics. Factor analysis is important in the field of individual
differences since, for the last few decades, it has been the most
popular tool-of-all-trades among psychometrists. In addition to
being used as an aid to the classifying of tests, it has been employed for purposes of test construction, validation and also for
'discovering' what it is that particular tests are assessing.

K. *illustrations of contexts and scoring from the Word-in-context test (p. 47)*

Contexts for GODOWN

On the way to the Quai Mytho I passed several ambulances driving out
of Cholon heading for the Place Garnier. One could almost reckon the
pace of rumour from the expression of the faces in the street, which at
first turned on someone like myself coming from the direction of the
Place with looks of expectancy and speculation. By the time I entered
Cholon I had outstripped the news: life was busy, normal, uninter-
rupted: nobody knew.

I found Mr Chou's godown and mounted to Mr Chou's house.
Nothing had changed since my last visit. The cat and dog moved from
floor to cardboard box to suitcase like a couple of chess knights who
cannot get to grips. The baby crawled on the floor, and the two old
men were still playing Mah-jongg. Only the young people were absent.
As soon as I appeared in the doorway one of the women began to pour
out tea. The old lady sat on the bed and looked at her feet.

Graham Greene, *The Quiet American*, Heinemann, 1955, p. 224

Of course, this thought was not clear in my mind at that time. Then and for
years after, my idea of fate – for in fate I firmly believed – was of a vague,
floating, stupendous power, for which I felt only resentful wonder.

Another puzzle came one midsummer airing day. It seems odd that
it should have happened then, for airing days were the most carefree,
happy time of the year for me. Then the godowns were emptied and

*Burt, C., *The Factors of the Mind*, University of London Press, 1940.
†Vernon, P. E., *The Structure of Human Abilities*, Methuen, 1950.

long ropes stretched in the sunshine, on which were hung torn banners bearing our crest, old field-curtains used in the camps of our ancestors, ancient regalia of house officers, and many odd-shaped garments belonging to what Ishi's fairy tales called 'the olden, olden time'. Beneath the low eaves were piles of clumsy horse armour bound with faded ropes of twisted silk; and old war weapons – spears, battle-axes, bows, and sheaves of arrows – stood in out-of-the-way corners of the garden. All available space was utilised; even the bridge-posts and the stone lanterns were decorated with chain-silk armour and lacquer helmets with fearful masks.

> Etsu Inagaki Sugimoto, *A Daughter of the Samurai*,
> Hurst and Blackett, 1933, p. 138

We berthed towards sunrise in a gloomy and featureless roadstead, before a town whose desolate silhouette suggested that of a tin-mining village in the Andes. An unlovely straggle of godowns, patched and peeling, fronted the shallow and dirty shore. Here and there along the flat coastline with its unhealthy suggestion of salt-pans (I was not wrong: Limassa lies upon a shallow lake), here and there the eye picked out a villa of some style or consequence in a flowering garden. But even at this early hour the sunlight created a dense haze while the humid air of the little port came out across the still sea to meet us.

> Lawrence Durrell, *Bitter Lemons*, Faber and Faber, 1957, p. 22

Scoring

Test-word: GODOWN (store or warehouse in the far East).

Final
verdict
score

5 (i) Store or warehouse.
  (ii) Some sort of store or warehouse – generally used of a rather ramshackle place.

4 (i) A shed or similar resting place for collected paraphernalia.
  (ii) Some sort of building. Perhaps a shed or storehouse.

3 (i) A building attached to a large dwelling, peculiar to Japan, serving the same function as an English junk-room.
  (ii) Old hut for living or storage.

2 (i) Barn or shack.
  (ii) A shed, out-house or hut.

1 (i) Beach hut (or Eastern equivalent).
  (ii) Rubbish bins, sometimes found in public places obviously customary and in no way to be looked down on though not necessarily decorative – just to serve their purpose.

0 (i) Apartment block.
  (ii) Slum doss-house.

−1 (i) American slang to mean street.
  (ii) Latrine.

−2 (i) Boat.
  (ii) A painted sort of cart for transporting people – an open vehicle.

Thus it may be seen that the answers scoring 5 have absolutely the right idea and only the right idea. 4 is still correct but slightly less definite and 3, again, is a degree less good.

Answers scoring 2 make no implicit mention of storing, or its equivalent, and those scoring 1 may not even imply this.

0 answers are positively mistaken but they still indicate some sort of building. —1 answers are not even buildings and —2s are not even stationary.

L. *level of difficulty* (*p. 64*)

The concept of level of difficulty is less simple than may appear at first sight. All would agree that certain tasks or problems are harder than others but not everybody realizes that what is the harder of two problems for one person may be the easier of the two problems for another. This is one of the reasons, sometimes unrecognized, for the difficulty in reaching agreement as to the meaning of the word 'intelligence'. Indeed this particular difference among people is one of the most frequent grounds for outspoken intolerance: 'But it's so *easy*!' exclaims an exasperated mathematics master to his sixth-form pupil – who writes, perhaps, clearer and livelier English than he does himself.

The same individual differences are found in intelligence tests and not only as between different biases. For instance, some Subjects find diagrammatic analogies easier than diagrammatic series and some find the latter easier. Psychometrists have taken the line that they should concern themselves with what is harder/easier for the group as a whole; that they must use an objective criterion. The most frequently used measure is the proportion of the group giving the correct solution to an item. Thus if 58 per cent get question 12 right and 49 per cent get question 13 right, question 12 is inferred to be easier than question 13.

It is occasionally recognized that the time taken to produce an answer can also be taken as a criterion of level of difficulty – though here again considerable individual variation occurs. This criterion is not often used as it demands the timing of individual responses to individual questions. This is not easy to do in a group test situation. Moreover it poses the question of whether the time taken to produce *any* answer should be the measure, or the time taken to produce *the correct* answer.

When the time taken over an item is used as the criterion, it is often assumed that it tallies with the other measure, namely that of the proportion of Subjects answering correctly. An experiment conducted on these matters,* however, suggests (*a*) that the two criteria do not necessarily coincide and (*b*) that Subjects' approach to multiple-choice questions may differ in this respect from that to open-ended questions.

M. g (p. 72)

The term *g* was coined by Spearman,† one of the most influential figures in British intelligence testing. *g* has gradually come to be used by psychometrists and others as synonymous with intelligence. Spearman, however, used the term to designate briefly

*Cane, V. R., and Horn, V., 'The timing of responses to spatial perception questions', *Quart. J. exper. Psychol.*, 3, 1951, 133–45.

†Spearman, C., *The Nature of Intelligence and the Principles of Cognition*, Macmillan, 1923.

(a) the fact that performances on various types of cognitive tasks tend to intercorrelate positively and (b) the workings of his three 'noegenetic principles'. He expressed these principles as follows:

1. *Apprehension of Experience.* 'Any lived experience tends to evoke immediately a knowing of its characters and experiencer.'

2. *Eduction of Relations.* 'The mentally presenting of any two or more characters (simple or complex) tends to evoke immediately a knowing of relations between them.'

3. *Eduction of Correlates.* 'The presenting of any character together with any relation tends to evoke immediately a knowing of the correlative character.'

The first of these appears to be an (over)statement of the fact of introspection. It is, in any case, not very relevant to the devising of test items. The second and third constitute examples of types of deductive reasoning. An illustration of the second would be educing the relation 'opposite' in response to the datum SOFT/HARD. An illustration of the third would be the eduction of the correlate 'hard' in response to the datum SOFT/relation OPPOSITE.

Spearman's principles of noegenesis are quoted here because the last two have formed the basis of most intelligence tests since Spearman's time and he attached very great importance to them. 'They, and they alone,' he wrote 'are generative of new items in the field of cognition.' This again would now be generally regarded as an overstatement – in the assumptions both of exclusiveness and comprehensiveness. For a fuller discussion of Spearman's views on noegenesis, see Heim's *The Appraisal of Intelligence*, pages 13–19.

N. *statistically unsatisfactory* (p. 80)

The statistical satisfactoriness of a multiple-choice test item depends mainly on two factors: (a) the capacity of the item to effect differentiation among the Subjects and (b) a reasonable degree of similarity, in what is being differentiated, between the item in question and the other items comprising the test.

Thus, an item is statistically unsatisfactory, (*a*) (i) if it is too easy for the relevant Subjects, i.e. if too high a proportion of them get the question right; (ii) if it is too difficult for the Subjects, i.e. if the proportion getting it right is only marginally better than chance; (iii) if one or more of the six proffered solutions is never chosen – thus effectively reducing the choice to one from five (or even one from four, or less) instead of one from six.

An item is statistically unsatisfactory (*b*) if those Subjects who answer it correctly obtain a *lower* score on the test as a whole than do those Subjects who answer the item incorrectly: i.e. each item should correlate positively and significantly with the other test items. The correlation need not be very high. In the present writer's opinion, it is a sign of healthy variety in a test if the inter-item correlation is *not* very high. If, on the other hand, the correlation be negative or around zero, the addition of scores gained on the various test-items becomes meaningless.

O. ipsative (pp. 96 and 104)

Most tests of personality, and all tests specifically of interests, with which the writer is acquainted (apart from the Brook) have 'ipsative' scoring, that is, the scores of a Subject are expressed in terms of deviation from his own mean. This stems from the tests being multiple-choice and forced-choice in form; from the psychometrist's passive acceptance of the difficulty of comparing the interest of one Subject with that of another Subject, since the depth and width of interest among Subjects may vary greatly; and from the psychometrist's belief – not always justified – that he can validly compare degree of interest *intra* Subject. This means he believes that for any given Subject, S, he can compare S's degree of interest in Aesthetics, say, with his degree of interest in Religion, and both of these with his interest, for instance, in Politics.

With ipsative scoring, if a Subject scores highly on several of the interests, he will automatically score low on the others. If, on the other hand, he gains an average score on all but one of the interests catered for – because he is moderately interested in them – he is bound to obtain an average score also on the last interest. Three Subjects, one of whom has little or no interest in the test categories, another of whom has a moderate interest in all – or all but one – of the test categories, and a third who is keenly interested in all the relevant categories, will gain identical, flat test profiles. Thus it is built into ipsative scoring (*a*) that the comparison of one individual's interest profile with another is not very meaningful and (*b*) that the profile of any one Subject is constrained to a considerable extent by the system of scoring.

A non-ipsative system of scoring allows for more meaningful intra-Subject comparison as well as for inter-Subject comparison. Furthermore it does not proscribe the Subject with wide interests from having some exceptionally high interest scores nor does it automatically ensure that Subjects with rather shallow interests will appear to spread them widely. Such a scoring system, however, will necessarily be based on open-ended questions, allowing free rein to the Subject.

P. neurotic and psychotic (*p. 97*)

Fairly close agreement obtains as to the distinction between neurosis and psychosis. Both indicate some degree of psychological disturbance but the psychotic is in general more severely ill than the neurotic and he tends also to have a different *kind* of disorder. Thus the psychotic is often said to be 'out of touch with reality'; to show, in many cases, deterioration in his thinking and cognitive processes generally; his expression of emotion may be grossly inappropriate or it may be 'flattened'; he may have hallucinations or delusions; he lacks 'insight' into his condition, typically refusing to seek, or submit to, medical treatment, on the grounds that there is nothing wrong with him. In fact, we say 'psychotic' to-day where yesterday we would have said 'insane' or 'mad'.

The neurotic, on the other hand, remains 'in touch with reality'; his thought processes are affected relatively little; his emotions may be somewhat exaggerated or diminished but they are understandable in the context in which he finds himself; he is apt to be over-anxious or over-obsessional, hypochondriacal or fearful; he has 'insight' in the sense that he is aware that he is unwell – indeed he will often go from doctor to doctor, convinced that his intense sufferings are almost unique and that nobody really understands him.

Thus a clear distinction between psychosis and neurosis can be drawn theoretically and can be comfortably maintained in many specific cases of psychiatric patients. There is, however, a tendency among some psychiatrists nowadays to see the distinction as less clearcut, for several reasons. First, the criterion of greater *severity* in psychosis does not always hold. Some cases of very serious neurosis are more incapacitating than are some mild cases of what are, on other grounds, diagnosed as psychosis. Secondly, a number of psychiatric symptoms – such as depression, alcoholism, paranoia – occur in 'normals', in 'neurotics' and in 'psychotics'. *Here* the diagnosis is determined mainly by the degree of severity of the disturbance.

Thirdly, the old classification of endogenous/reactive is gradually disappearing as it is realized that in the majority of breakdowns, both innate constitution and past or present environmental stress, play their part. Everyone has his breaking point. Some are tougher and some are constitutionally more sensitive, but all will show some signs of disturbance if exposed for long enough to sufficiently intense strain. If this is the case: if the outcome depends on the *balance* of the individual's psycho-physical constitution and his environment, then a clear cut distinction between normality, neurosis and psychosis becomes untenable.

Q. K = practical (p. 100)

The symbol K was chosen to represent interest in *Practical* matters in the Brook Reaction test because there are already two interest categories beginning with a P (*People* and *Political*) and K is the symbol used for psychometric tests of spatial perception and practical ability. It may appear strange to identify good spatial perception with good practical ability but this seems to be one of the psychometric findings which has been repeatedly confirmed.

K tests assess the Subject's capacity to manipulate mentally different shapes and sizes, drawn two-dimensionally and three-dimensionally. These tests include such problems as estimating how many times a given small figure must be used to make up a larger figure, imagining how a particular figure will look if it be turned over and/or round, and determining how a line should be drawn through a given figure in order that its two parts should make up a square. It is thus, primarily, a test of rather specialized visual imagery.

K tests have been found useful in predicting success in such occupations as engineering, carpentry and dressmaking. But they have also been found to correlate with a general characteristic of 'practicality', interpreting this in the broadest way. Thus people who do well on *K* tests tend also to be good at solving practical problems, whether they involve starting a recalcitrant motor-car, repairing an adjustable clothes-airer or paper-hanging. On the other hand, people who score poorly on *K* tests tend to perform poorly when faced with practical problems. The latter tend also to lack *interest* in practical problems – though whether the hen or the egg comes first here is hard to say.

It has been found in the Brook Reaction test that a high *K* interest score (as well as a high *Physical Science* score) tends to go with good examination results in G.C.E. A-level physics and mathematics. This would confirm (*a*) the well-known phenomenon that interest and ability go together generally (although there are notable exceptions) and (*b*) that the Brook *K* score gives a good measure of degree of interest in matters that have practical implications.

R. halo effect (p. 112)

'Halo effect' signifies the tendency one has, when assessing the characteristics of other people, to be influenced unwittingly by the impression they have made on one in respect of *other* characteristics. It includes two phenomena*: (*a*) the tendency to base one's total judgement about a person on some one strong *particular* impression; and (*b*) the tendency to allow a strong *general* impression to colour all judgements concerning the Subject's specific qualities.

S. correction for attenuation (*p. 114*)

Psychometrists sometimes 'correct test correlations for attenuation'. This has the effect of raising the correlation coefficient, the argument being that the correlation found is lower than that which would be obtained between 'true scores'.† The most frequent cases in which such 'correction' is done are (*a*) those in which the Subjects form a highly homogeneous group, such as university students, for instance, or – at the other end of the scale – mental defectives and (*b*) those in which one (or more) of the tests has low consistency.

Whilst it is true that testing in these conditions does tend to lower the relevant correlations, their boosting by means of such 'correction' is not defensible. It would be easy enough to produce a highly inconsistent test, T1, and correct its correlation with test T2 so that their 'true scores' would correlate highly – even perhaps in excess of unity! But this is a good deal less than satisfactory. If a test is inconsistent, the test should itself be improved until it yields consistent results. If a test is intended for a highly selected sample, it is no use calculating what a high correlation it would yield with a random sample. As McNemar says:

Correlation coefficients corrected for attenuation are of theoretical importance in the analysis of relationships in that allowance can be made for variable errors of measurement, but such corrected *r's* are of little practical value since they cannot be used in prediction equations.

*Heim, A. W., 'Industrial assessments: some problems and suggestions', *Occup. Psychol.*, **20**, 1946, 24–33.

† McNemar, Q., *Psychological Statistics*, Chapman and Hall, 1949, 134–46.

The prediction of one variable from another and the acompanying error of estimate must necessarily be based on obtained, or fallible, rather than true scores.

My only quarrel with this is the assumption that 'true score' has a meaning and that the scores gained on an inconsistent test can by means of a statistical technique be rendered closer to the truth.

T. construct validation (*pp. 36 and 122*)

In this note, as in the text, quotations are used in view of the extreme difficulty of attaining any clear understanding of the concept of 'construct validation'. Anstey writes:*

By construct validity is meant demonstrating that 'certain explanatory constructs or intervening variables (such as intelligence, authoritarianism, or extraversion-introversion) account to some degree for performance in the test'. Some external evidence is necessary also, and the construct must be submitted to objective confirmation.

This looks fine until one asks oneself (*a*) just *how* the explanatory constructs are demonstrated to account for test performance and (*b*) just what constitutes the additional 'objective confirmation' to which Anstey refers. Perhaps the last word should be left to Kelly† who spells out some of the difficulties of construct validation:

Most present day personality theories are so nonrigorous in the definitions of their constructs and in their explication of necessary relationships among them that there is as yet tragically little consensus regarding either key trait constructs or the best methods of assessing them. Instead, we find, as has already been noted, the confusing situation whereby Investigators A and B may each develop (and even market!) a purported test of Construct X, but subsequent application of the two tests to the same group reveals no more than chance relationships

*Anstey, E., *Psychological Tests*, Nelson, 1966.
†Kelly, E. Lowell, *Assessment of Human Characteristics*, Basic Concepts in Psychology Series, Wadsworth Publishing Company, New York, 1967.

between the two sets of measures. Obviously, both tests cannot have construct validity for the same construct. For scientists, such a finding points to one of three possible conclusions:

1. A's test measures Construct X, or
2. B's test measures Construct X, or
3. Neither test measures Construct X.

Only through further investigations to determine the relationships of both sets of scores to a wide variety of behaviors is it possible to choose between these three mutually exclusive possibilities.

Alternatively, as we have also noted, two assessment techniques may purport to measure different constructs, yet the measures which they yield correlate as highly as the reliabilities of the two sets of scores will permit. Confronted with this unfortunate and all too common situation, the scientist has a choice of two conclusions:

1. Construct X is the same as Construct Y, in spite of the fact that the two bear a different label and may have a different theoretical basis, or
2. Both techniques are measuring the same construct, but perhaps a different one, Construct Z!

Again, the choice between these alternative conclusions must await the accumulation of further research evidence. In the long run, the question 'What does a test measure?' must be answered in terms of a continuing analysis of the correlations of its scores with as many other different measures and criteria as possible. Each such newly discovered relationship is potentially helpful in sharpening the *true* meaning of any set of test scores – in other words, their construct validity.

U. adequate stimulus (p. 128)

By an 'adequate stimulus' is meant an *appropriate* stimulus. Thus the adequate stimulus for vision, for instance, is light energy and the adequate stimulus for hearing is sound energy. The stimulus must, of course, be intense enough to be seen, heard or smelt, etc. but the word 'adequate' in this context is used to refer to appropriateness of stimulus to sense organ rather than intensity or magnitude of stimulus.

The term has been coined because it is possible to gain visual and other sensations from 'inadequate' stimuli. For example, the passing of a slight electric current through the temples gives rise to the sight of short, white flashes on the part of the Subject; a mechanical stimulus, such as a blow on the head, will produce the well-known phenomenon of 'seeing stars'. Again, in the auditory field, the vibrations of a pneumatic drill may be experienced as pain rather than as sound.

V. negative transfer (p. 129)

When the possession of one skill results in the facilitation of acquiring a second skill, this is known as 'positive transfer'. Consider, for instance, somebody who has played the piano for some years and who now wishes to learn to use a typewriter. She (or he) will usually learn to type more easily and quickly than will non-pianists of similar age, intelligence, education and keenness. This is readily understandable since both skills require the capacity to 'send messages to' separate fingers, to move them while looking elsewhere and to work rhythmically. Similarly there is strong positive transfer between playing the violin and playing the viola. The player will naturally at first feel put off by the larger scale of the viola but he will perform far better in a short time than he would have if starting without previous experience on the violin.

Positive transfer occurs too in operating certain machines such as capstan lathes, centre lathes and milling machines. It is found to some extent also among games, such as card games and ball games. But *negative* transfer may occur among ball games which are sufficiently similar 'to put one off'. People who play tennis in the Summer and squash in the Winter, for example, often find that they are using their wrist too much at the beginning of Summer (negative transfer from squash to tennis) and using their shoulder and arm too much at the beginning of the Winter (negative transfer from tennis to squash).

Another example of negative transfer is in the learning of Italian and Spanish, simultaneously. Whilst there is some positive transfer in language-learning generally – the more languages one knows, the easier it is to acquire yet another – Italian and Spanish are so much alike that they are apt to confuse the learner. This does not happen if the student is learning simultaneously Italian and German, for instance, since these two languages are sufficiently different not to interfere with each other.

W. amnesia (p. 130)

'Amnesia' is a technical term for forgetting. But it is not strictly synonymous with 'forgetting', for it carries with it a suggestion of *abnormal* forgetting or of failing to recall in circumstances where recall is to be expected. The term, however, is used also in unusual circumstances where forgetting is indeed the rule rather than the exception. Thus one may read that 'amnesia usually follows on concussion' or that 'some measure of amnesia is common after electro-convulsive therapy'.

Amnesia may be selective. It may affect, for instance, a patient's ability to remember names: these may be proper names such as Jennifer or Churchill and/or names of objects such as 'comb' or 'pencil'. Amnesia is not, however, confined to nouns or even to words. The forgetting of one's own previous experience may also be referred to as amnesia, especially when it is dramatic or unexpected.

In the 'fugues' occasionally reported in the press, whole sections of a person's previous life may be forgotten and he may be unable to recall his name, marital status, place of abode, etc. Such failures of memory may be total or partial; they may be temporary or permanent. When they are temporary they may be referred to as 'amnesic periods' or 'episodes'.

X. lack of insight (p. 131)

'Insight' is one of the many words used both by the psychologist and the layman with a good deal of overlap in meaning. For both of them it signifies essentially *understanding*. But when the layman uses the term, he generally has in mind acumen, perceptiveness, discernment; i.e. his connotation is a very broad one which takes in all the various aspects and implications of 'understanding'.

The psychologist, on the other hand, uses the term more narrowly and it has for him two slightly differing meanings. Let us consider first the meaning in the text, as in 'the lack of insight of the truly senile'. Such lack of insight refers specifically to the fact that the truly senile will usually not realize that there is anything wrong with them. It is in this sense that a psychologist may say of a psychotic patient that 'he has no insight' – meaning that the patient will deny that he is ill. This does, of course, signify a lack of understanding but it is of a specific kind.

The second psychological meaning of 'insight' is that used, for instance, by Köhler in *The Mentality of Apes*, to designate the sudden and correct solution of problems, based on perception of the relevant relationships, as opposed to solution by trial and error (or by mechanical conditioning). When the problem-solver is human, it is sometimes, though not always, possible to ascertain whether insight in this sense determined the solution, by an appeal to introspection. Such problem-solving is sometimes picturesquely called 'the aha! phenomenon'.

When, however, the problem-solver is one of the lower animals, those psychologists who believe that these are capable of insight use such criteria as the following, to determine whether insight has played a part in reaching the solution: a sudden drop in the learning curve (as opposed to the classical gradual drop, in time taken to solve the problem); immediate success in tackling the same, or similar, problems on subsequent occasions; flexibility in means, while going clearly for the same end (e.g. an ape may use his left hand having previously used his right, if the latter is out of action); manifestation of joyous high spirits on the part of the animal when he solves the problem.

Y. *perseverative* (*p. 132*)

To be 'perseverative' (or to have a high degree of 'perseveration') is not the same thing as to be persevering. The latter is a term,

familiar to everyone, which signifies the trait traditionally attributed to Robert Bruce, who is said to have 'tried and tried again'.
'Perseverance' thus denotes diligence, persistence and effort in
the face of failure. But the term 'perseveration' has been coined
by psychologists to signify a tendency to continue with the same
mode of activity (or feeling or idea) after it has ceased to be
appropriate: to find it difficult suddenly to change one's approach
to a task or to change from one task to another.

Tests of perseveration are thought to give some indication of
the Subject's degree of rigidity: an index of the ease with which he
can switch from one mode of reaction to another. The tasks set
can be either simple performance tests or abstract problem-
solving situations. The former may be exemplified by asking the
Subject to write as many rows of Ss as he can in, say, one minute
(S S S . . .); then asking him to produce as many mirror-image Ss
(Ƨ Ƨ Ƨ . . .) as he can in a second minute; and, finally, to produce
as many ordinary Ss as possible in a third minute.

There is a well-known schoolboy joke which offers an example
of a verbal test of perseveration. The boy asks his friend, 'How
do you pronounce M–A–C–D–E–R–M–O–T–T?' (pause for reply);
'And how do you pronounce M–A–C–F–A–R–L–A–N–E?' (pause for
reply); 'And how do you pronounce M–A–C–D–O–N–A–L–D?' (pause
for reply); 'And how do you pronounce M–A–C–H–I–N–E–R–Y?'
This works better orally than visually.

The phenomenon of 'perseveration' can be observed also in
more complex problem-solving. For example, in questions of the
pint-jar filling type it has been shown* that if the Subject is given,
say, five consecutive problems all of which demand that the
smaller of two jars be filled first, he is likely to 'perseverate' and
suggest filling first the smaller of two jars in a sixth, far easier,
problem – where it is obvious to a fresh Subject that first filling
the larger jar will immediately yield the solution. This type of
obstructive habit-formation is often experienced in real-life
situations.

*Luchins, A. S., 'Mechanization in problem solving', *Psychol. Monogr.*,
54, 1942, No. 248.

Notes

Z. mean score (p. 136)

The 'mean score' on a test is the average score. It is the result
obtained by adding together all the scores gained by the Subjects
comprising a test group and dividing that total by the number of
Subjects in the group. There are, however, other types of average
score, notably the 'mode' and the 'median'. The mode is, as the
term suggests, the most popular or frequently gained score. The
median is that score which has as many Subjects scoring above it
as below it.

FIGURE 6A

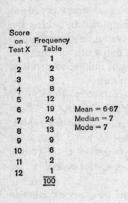

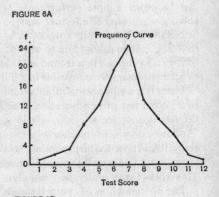

Score on Test X	Frequency Table		
1	1		
2	2		
3	3		
4	8		
5	12		
6	19	Mean = 6·67
7	24	Median = 7
8	13	Mode = 7
9	9		
10	6		
11	2		
12	1		
	100		

FIGURE 6B

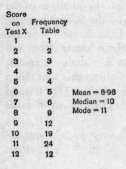

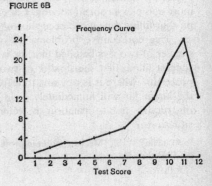

Score on Test X	Frequency Table		
1	1		
2	2		
3	3		
4	3		
5	4		
6	5	Mean = 8·96
7	6	Median = 10
8	9	Mode = 11
9	12		
10	19		
11	24		
12	12		

186

When the frequency distribution of a test is 'normal', these three measures coincide. This is shown in Figure 6(a), where each of the three averages equals approximately 7·0. Where, however, the frequency distribution is skewed, the mean, mode and median may yield three different values. An example of this is shown in Figure 6(b), where, it may be seen, the mean = 9·0, the mode = 11·0 and the median = 10·0. All these averages are approximate. For both these hypothetical examples, the number in the group is 100.

AA. spatial problems (p. 138)

Spatial problems assess the Subject's ability to manipulate mentally two- and three-dimensional figures (see Note Q). Performance tests of spatial perception also exist. In such tests the Subject is allowed to pick up and handle the (wooden or cardboard) shapes, in order to fit them into their appropriately-shaped slots, instead of being confined exclusively to visual imagery.

BB. anthropormorphism (p. 150)

Anthropormorphism is one of the greatest sins which, in the behaviourist's view, other behaviourists can commit. It consists of attributing to the lower animals thoughts and feelings which – obviously – cannot be directly observed. Either the behaviourist denies the existence of such phenomena generally (or claims that we should behave as though they did not exist) in the interests of scientific objectivity; or, in the same interests, he objects to the attribution of such characteristics to the lower animals since (a) these, lacking language, cannot confirm or deny the hypothetical experiences and (b) once the existence of such thoughts or feelings (however clearly demonstrated) is accepted, where will it end? Paradoxically, however, experimental psychologists are becoming increasingly anthropormorphic about their machines. These are said to think, to experience, to predict and to learn – all without quotation marks!

CC. ethologists (p. 153)

'Ethologist' resembles 'animal psychologist' in that both work with the lower animals as their Subjects, both have a scientific approach and both, therefore, make use of the experimental method. But whereas the animal psychologist does laboratory experiments – and, in so doing, often submits his Subjects to singularly inappropriate experimental situations – the ethologist observes the animal in its natural environment and also conducts experiments mainly in conditions which have some bearing on the animal's normal life.

Thus the psychologist manipulates his animals, imposing essentially human values and goals upon them, and he draws his conclusions from the somewhat artificial data so obtained – often making doubtful extrapolations from rats or other animals to human beings. The ethologist, on the other hand, studies his animals as they develop in natural, or near-natural, conditions and adopts the attitude that he may have something to learn from the interactions among Subjects or between Subjects and their environment.

It has been said, facetiously, that the main difference between the two groups is that 'the ethologists like their animals' and the animal psychologists do not. Certainly the major ethologists (such as Tinbergen, Lorenz, Hinde and Thorpe) appear to empathize and even sometimes to identify with their Subjects in a way that experimental psychologists deliberately do not.

References

Chapter One

1 Warren, H. C., *Dictionary of Psychology*, Houghton Mifflin, New York, 1934.
2 Drever, J., *A Dictionary of Psychology*, Penguin, 1952.
3 Watson, J. B., *Psychology from the Standpoint of a Behaviorist*, Lippincott, Philadelphia, 1924.

Chapter Two

1a Burt, C., 'The Genetic Determination of Differences in Intelligence: a Study of Monozygotic Twins Reared Together and Apart', *British Journal of Psychology*, **57**, 1966, 137–53.
b Stott, D. H., 'Commentary on "The Genetic Determination of Differences in Intelligence: a Study of Monozygotic Twins Reared Together and Apart" by Cyril Burt: Congenital Influences on the Development of Twins', *British Journal of Psychology*, **57**, 1966, 423–29.
c Lewis, D. G., 'Commentary on "The Genetic Determination of Differences in Intelligence: a Study of Monozygotic Twins Reared Together and Apart" by Cyril Burt', *British Journal of Psychology*, **57**, 1966, 431–33.
d Newman, H. H., *Twins and Supertwins*, Hutchinson, London, 1942.
e Woodworth, R. S., 'Heredity and Environment: A Critical Survey of Recently Published Material on Twins and Foster-children', *Social Research Council Bulletin*, No. 47, 1941.
2 Levine, S., 'The Effects of Infantile Experience on Adult Behavior', in Bachrach, A. J., (ed). *Experimental Foundations of Clinical Psychology*, Basic Books, New York, 1962.
3 Beach, F. A., and Jaynes, J., 'Effects of Early Experience upon the Behaviour of Animals', *Psychological Bulletin*, **51**, 1954, 239–63.
4 See Heim, A. W., *The Appraisal of Intelligence*, Methuen, 1954. New edn 1970, N.F.E.R., Chapter 12.

References

5a See, e.g., Terman, L. M., Thorndike, E. L., Thurstone, LL., *et. al.* 'Intelligence and Its Measurement: A Symposium', *Journal of Educational Psychology*, **12**, 1921, 123–54; 195–216.

b Miles, T. R., 'Contributions to Intelligence Testing and the Theory of Intelligence. I. On Defining Intelligence', *British Journal of Educational Psychology*, **27**, 1957,153–65.

6 Burt, C. L., 'The Evidence for the Concept of Intelligence', *British Journal of Educational Psychology*, **25**, 1955, 158–77.

7 Hebb, D. O., *The Organization of Behaviour*, Chapman and Hall, 1949.

8 Miles, *op. cit.* 5b.

9 Wechsler, D., *The Measurement of Adult Intelligence*, Williams and Wilkins, Baltimore, 1944.

10a Binet, A., and Simon, T. H., *Method of Measuring the Development of the Intelligence of Young Children*, Chicago Medical Book Company, 1915.

b Terman, L. M., and Merrill, M. A., *Measuring Intelligence*, Harrap, 1937.

11 Terman, Thorndike, Thurstone, *et al.*, *op cit*. 5a.

12 Heim, *op. cit.*, 4, Chapter III.

Chapter Three

1 Anstey, E., *Psychological Tests*, Nelson, 1966, 60–172.

2 Wiseman, S., (ed.), *Intelligence and Ability*, Penguin, 1967.

Chapter Four

1 Guilford, J. P., 'Creativity', *American Psychologist*, 5, 1950, 444–54.

2a Getzels, J. W., and Jackson, P. W., *Creativity and Intelligence*, Wiley, New York, 1962.

b Tyson, M., 'Creativity', in Foss, B. M., (ed.), *New Horizons in Psychology*, Penguin, 1966, 167–82.

c McClelland, D. C., 'On the Psychodynamics of Creative Physical Scientists', in Gruber, H. E., (ed.), *Contempory Approaches to Creative Thinking*, Atherton, New York, 1962.

3 Guilford, J. P., *et. al.*, 'A Factor Analytic Study of Creative Thinking II: Administration of Tests and Analysis of Results', *Reports from the Psychology Laboratory*, No. 8, University of Southern California, Los Angeles, 1952.

4 Cattell, R. B., *Objective-Analytic Test Battery*, Institute for Personality and Ability Testing, Champaign, Illinois, 1956.

5 Hasan, P., and Butcher, H. J., 'Creativity and Intelligence: a Partial Replication with Scottish Children of Getzels and Jackson's Study', *British Journal of Psychology*, **57**, 1966, 129–35.

6 Hudson, L., *Contrary Imaginations*, Methuen, 1966, Penguin, 1969.

7 *Nuffield Foundation Science Teaching Project*, (Secondary), Longmans/Penguin, 1967.
Nuffield Foundation Science Teaching Project, (Junior), Collins, 1967.
Nuffield Mathematics Project, Chambers and Murray, J., for The Nuffield Foundation, 1967.

8 Meier, N. C., *Art Judgment Test*, Bureau of Educational Research and Service, University of Iowa, 1940.

9 Heim, A. W., *The Appraisal of Intelligence*, Methuen, 1954. New edn 1970, N.F.E.R.

Chapter Five

1 Cook, J. M., Heim, A. W., and Watts, K. P., 'The Word-in-context: a New Type of Verbal Reasoning Test', *British Journal of Psychology*, **54**, 1963, 227–37.

2 Heim, A. W., and Watts, K. P., 'A Preliminary Study of the Self-judging Vocabulary Scale', *British Journal of Psychology*, **52**, 1961, 175–86.

3 Heim, A. W., 'Psychological Testing and its Uses', *Conference*, 1966.

4 Alcock, T., *The Rorschach in Practice*, Tavistock, 1963.

5 See, e.g., Werner, H., 'Change of Meaning: a Study of Semantic Processes through the Experimental Method', *Journal of General Psychology*, **50**, 1954, 181–208.

6a Glaze, J. A., 'The Association Value of Nonsense Syllables', *Journal of Genetic Psychology*, **35**, 1928, 225–67.

b Conrad, R., 'Practice, Familiarity and Reading Rate for Words and Nonsense Syllables', *Quarterly Journal of Experimental Psychology*, **14**, 1962, 71–6.

7a Cook, Heim and Watts, *op. cit*.

b Heim, A. W., Povey, R. M., and Watts, K. P., 'An Attempt to Measure Some Aspects of Temperament by Means of the Word-in-context and Self-judging Vocabulary Tests', *Journal of General Psychology*, **72**, 1965, 285–94.

References

c Salmon, P., Bramley, J., and Presly, A. S., 'The Word-in-context as a Measure of Conceptualization in Schizophrenics with and without Thought Disorder', *British Journal of Medical Psychology*, **40**, 1967 253-9.

8 Povey, R. M., 'Arts/Science Differences: Their Relationship to Curriculum Specialization', *British Journal of Psychology*, **61**, 1970, 55-64.

9 Frenkel-Brunswik, E., 'Intolerance of Ambiguity as an Emotional and Perceptual Personality Variable', *Journal of Personality*, **18**, 1949, 108-43.

10 Schafer, R., 'The Expression of Personality and Maladjustment in Intelligence Test Results', in Semeonoff, B., (ed.), *Personality Assessment*, Penguin Modern Psychology, 1966.

Chapter Six

1 Allport, G. W., *Personality: a Psychological Interpretation*, Holt, New York, 1937.

2a Vernon, P. E., *Personality Assessment: A Critical Survey*, Methuen, 1964.

b Semeonoff, B., (ed.), *Personality Assessment*, Penguin, 1966.

3 Hathaway, S. R., and McKinley, J. C., *Minnesota Multiphasic Personality Inventory Manual*, Psychological Corporation, New York, 1951.

4 Heim, A. W., *The Appraisal of Intelligence*, Methuen, 1954. New edn 1970, N.F.E.R., Chapters 6 and 7.

5a Thomson, G., 'Intelligence and Civilization' in Wiseman, S., (ed.), *Intelligence and Ability*, Penguin, 1967, 115-30.

b Vernon, P. E., *The Structure of Human Abilities*, Methuen, 1950.

6 Masserman, J. H., *Behaviour and Neurosis*, University of Chicago and Cambridge University Press, 1943.

7a Maier, N. R. F., Glaser, N. M., and Klee, J. B., 'Studies of Abnormal Behaviour in the Rat: III The Development of Behavioural Fixations Through Frustration', *Journal of Experimental Psychology*, **26**, 1940, 521-46.

b Maier, N. R. F., *Frustration: A Study of Behavior without a Goal*, McGraw-Hill, New York, 1949.

8 Bruner, J. S., and Goodman, C. C., 'Value and Need as Organizing Factors in Perception', *Journal of Abnormal Psychology*, **42**, 1947, 33-44.

9 Carter, L. F., and Schooler, K., 'Value, Need and Other Factors in Perception', *Psychological Review*, 56, 1949, 200–7.

10 Heckhausen, H., *The History of Achievement Motivation*, Academic Press, New York, 1967.

11 Helson, H., 'Adaptation Level as a Basis for a Quantitative Theory of Frames of Reference', *Psychological Review*, LV, 1948, 297–313.

12 Mace, C. A., 'Incentives: Some Experimental Studies', *Report of Industrial Health Research Board*, 72, 1935.

13 Heim, A. W., 'Psychological Adaptation as a Response to Variations in Difficulty and Intensity', *Journal of General Psychology*, 56, 1957, 193–211.

14 Heim, A. W., 'Adaptation to Level of Difficulty in Intelligence Testing', *British Journal of Psychology*, 46, 1955, 211–24.

15 See, e.g., Furneaux, W. D., *Nufferno Tests of Speed and Level*, London University Press, 1956–1962.

16 Heim, A. W., Ramsay, B., and Watts, K. P., 'Adaptation to Level of Difficulty in Judging the Familiarity of Words', *British Journal of Educational Psychology*, 34, 1964, 109–19.

17 See, e.g., Frank, J. D., 'Recent Studies in Level of Aspiration', *Psychology Bulletin*, 38, 1941, 218–25.

Chapter Seven

1 Yates, A., Vernon, P. E., *et. al.* 'Symposium on the Effects of Coaching and Practice in Intelligence Tests', *British Journal of Educational Psychology*, 23/24, 1953/4.

2 Watts, K. P., 'Intelligence Test Performance from 11 to 18: a Study of Grammar School Girls', *British Journal of Educational Psychology*, 28, 1958, 112–9.

3a James, W. S., 'Coaching for All Recommended', *British Journal of Educational Psychology*, 23, 1953, 155–62.

b Dempster, J. J. B., 'Southampton Investigation and Procedure', *British Journal of Educational Psychology*, 24, 1954, 1–4.

4a Yates, A., 'An Analysis of Some Recent Investigations', *British Journal of Educational Psychology*, 23, 1953, 147–54.

b Wiseman, S., 'The Manchester Experiment', *British Journal of Educational Psychology*, 24, 1954, 5–8.

5 Rodger, A. G., 'The Application of Six Group Intelligence Tests to the Same Children, and the Effects of Practice', *British Journal of Educational Psychology*, 6, 1936, 291–305.

References

6a Thorndike, E. L., 'Practice Effects in Intelligence Tests', *Journal of Experimental Psychology*, **5**, 1922, 101–7.

 b Vernon, P. E., ' Intelligence Test Sophistication', *British Journal of Educational Psychology*, **8**, 1938, 237–44

7a McIntosh, D. M., 'The Effect of Practice in Intelligence Test Results', *British Journal of Educational Psychology*, **14**, 1944, 44–5.

 b McRae, E., 'The Inconstancy of Group Test I.Q.s', *British Journal of Educational Psychology*, **12**, 1942, 59–70.

8 Vernon, P. E., 'Conclusions of Symposium', *British Journal of Educational Psychology*, **24**, 1954, 57–63.

9 Heim, A. W., and Watts, K. P., 'An Experiment on Practice, Coaching and Discussion of Errors in Mental Testing', *British Journal of Educational Psychology*, **27**, 1957, 199–210.

10 Heim, A. W., and Simmonds, V., 'The Shapes Analysis, a Test of Spatial Perception', *Perceptual and Motor Skills*, **20**, 1965, 158.

11 Cane, V. R., and Horn, V., 'The Timing of Responses to Spatial Perception Questions', *Quarterly Journal of Experimental Psychology*, **3**, 1951, 133–45.

12a Heim, A. W., and Wallace, J. G., 'The Effects of Repeatedly Retesting the same Group on the same Intelligence Test. Part I: Normal Adults', *Quarterly Journal of Experimental Psychology*, **1**, 1949, 151–9.
  'Part II: High Grade Mental Defectives', *Quarterly Journal of Experimental Psychology*, **2**, 1949, 19–32.

 b Cane, V. R., and Heim, A. W., 'The Effects of Repeated Retesting: III Further Experiments and General Conclusions', *Quarterly Journal of Experimental Psychology*, **2**, 1950, 182–97.

13a Heim, A. W., *Manual for the Group Test of General Intelligence AH 4*, National Foundation for Educational Research, 1955, (Revised 1967).

 b Heim, A. W., *Manual for the Group Test of High-Grade Intelligence AH 5*, National Foundation for Educational Research, 1956, (Revised 1968).

Chapter Eight

1 See Anstey, E., *Psychological Tests*, Nelson, 1966, for a full Account of Item Analysis Methods and other techniques.

2 See, e.g., (a) Raven, J. C., *Progressive Matrices*, H. K. Lewis and

Co. Ltd., 1938. Often described as being 'very highly saturated with *g*'. (b) Penrose, L., *Pattern Perception Test*, 1947.

3 Robinson, C. A., and Nuttall, D. L., 'Is the Score on a Test of Spatial Perception Affected by the Subjects' Drawing on the Questions?' Psychological Laboratory, Cambridge, (unpublished).

4 Wallace, J. G., 'Results of a Test of High Grade Intelligence applied to a University Population', *British Journal of Psychology*, **43**, 1952, 61–9.

Chapter Nine

1a Heim, A. W., 'An Attempt to Test High Grade Intelligence', *British Journal of Psychology*, **37**, 1947, 70–81.

b Heim, A. W., and Batts, V., 'Upward and Downward Selection in Intelligence Testing', *British Journal of Psychology*, **39**, 1948, 22–9.

c Cronbach, L. J., *Essentials of Psychological Testing*, Harrap, New York, 1960, 221–3.

2a Vernon, P. E., *The Structure of Human Abilities*, Methuen, 1950.

b Burt, C., 'The Structure of the Mind: a Review of the Results of Factor Analysis', *British Journal of Educational Psychology*, **19**, 1949, 110 and 176.

3 Furneaux, W. D., *Nufferno Tests of Speed and Level*, London University Press, 1956.

4 Heim and Batts, *op. cit.*

Chapter Ten

1a Guilford, J. P., 'Intelligence: 1965 Model', *American Psychologist* **21**, 1966, 20–6.

b Guilford, J. P., 'Three Faces of Intellect', *American Psychologist*, **14**, 1959, 469–79.

2 Alcock, T., *The Rorschach in Practice*, Tavistock, 1963.

3 Lindzey, G., Bradford, J., Tejessy, C., and Davids, A., 'Thematic Apperception Test: An Interpretative Lexicon for Clinician and Investigator', *Journal of Clinical Psychology*, Monograph Supplement, No. 12, 1959.

4 Eysenck, H. J., *Eysenck Personality Inventory*, University of London Press, 1963.

5a Allport, G., Vernon, P. E., and Lindzey, G., *Study of Values*, Houghton Mifflin, 1931–60.

References

b British Edition: Richardson, S., *Study of Values*, National Foundation for Educational Research, 1965.

6 Weider, A., Wolff, H. G., Brodman, K., Mittelmann, B., and Wechsler, D., *Cornell Index*, Psychological Corporation, New York, 1948.

7 Hathaway, S. R., and McKinley, J. C., *Minnesota Multiphasic Personality Inventory*, Psychological Corporation, New York, 1942–51.

8 See, e.g., Messick, S., and Ross, J., (ed.) *Measurement in Personality and Cognition*, Wiley, New York, 1962.

9 Eysenck, H. J., and Eysenck, S. B. G., 'An Experimental Investigation of "Desirability" Response Set in a Personality Questionnaire', *Life Science*, 5, 1963, 343–55.

10 Eysenck, H.J. and Eysenck S. B. G., *Manual of the Eysenck Personality Inventory*, University of London Press, 1964, 12–13.

11 ibid., 16–17

12 Eysenck, H. J., *Maudsley Personality Inventory*, University of London Press, 1959–62.

13 Knapp, R. R., *Manual of the Maudsley Personality Inventory*. Educational and Industrial Testing Service, San Diego, 1962.

14 Buros, O. K., (ed.). *The Sixth Mental Measurements Yearbook* 1965, *see* Review by Lingoes, J. C.

15 Eysenck, H. J., 'The Biological Basis of Criminal Behaviour', *Advancement of Science*, London, 21, 1964, 338–48.

16a Allport, G. W., and Vernon, P. E., 'A Test of Personal Values', *Journal of Abnormal and Social Psychology*, 26, 1931, 231–48.

b Vernon, P. E., 'Questionnaires, Attitude Tests and Rating Scales', in Bartlett, F. C., *et. al.*, (ed.,) *The Study of Society*, Kegan Paul, 1939, Chapter IX.

17 Spranger, E., *Types of Men*. Translated from 5th German edition of *Lebensformen* by Pigors, P. J. W., Halle: Max Niemeyer Verlag. American agent: Stechert-Hafner, Inc., 31 East 10th Street, N.Y.3.

Chapter Eleven

1a Heim, A. W., Watts, K. P., and Simmonds, V., *Brook Reaction Test Manual*, National Foundation for Educational Research, 1970.

b Heim, A. W., and Watts, K. P., 'The Brook Reaction Test of Interests', *British Journal of Psychology*, 57, 1966, 171–85.

c Kline, P., 'The Validity of the Brook Reaction Test', *British Journal of Social and Clinical Psychology*, 9, 1970, 42–5.

2a Jung, C. G., *Studies in Word Association*, Heinemann, 1918.

b Kent, G. H., and Rosanoff, A. J., 'A Study of Association in Insanity', *American Journal of Insanity*, 67, 1910, 317–90.

c Burt, C., *The Subnormal Mind*, Oxford University Press, 1955, Chapter VIII and Appendix IV.

d Brown, W. P., 'Emotional Indicators in Word Association', *British Journal of Psychology*, 56, 1965, 401–12.

3 Brook, D. F. and Heim, A. W., 'A Preliminary Note on the Brook Reaction Test', *British Journal of Psychology*, 51, 1960, 347–56.

4 Hargreaves, D. H., Heim, A. W., and Watts, K. P., 'An Experiment on the Effects of Mental Set in the Brook Reaction Test', *British Journal of Educational Psychology*, 33, 1963, 236–9.

5a Burt, *op. cit.*

b Brown, *op. cit.*

6a Heim, A. W., Watts, K. P., and Simmonds, V., 'The Brook Reaction as a Test of Temperament', *British Journal of Social and Clinical Psychology*, 6, 1967, 304–12.

b Heim, A. W., 'The Brook Reaction as a Test of Interests and Temperament', *Occupational Psychology*, 42, 1968, 105–10.

7 Kline, P., 'The Reliability of the Brook Reaction Test', *British Journal of Social and Clinical Psychology*, 8, 1969, 83–4.

8 Heim, Watts and Simmonds, *op. cit.*, 1a.

9 Pear, T. H., 'Psychologists' and Novelists' Approaches to Personal Relations', *British Psychological Society Bulletin*, 20, 1967, No. 69.

Chapter Twelve

1 Patterson, J., *Personal Communication*, 1969.

2a Vernon, P. E., and Parry, J. B., *Personal Selection in the British Forces*, University of London Press, 1947.

b Heim, A. W., 'Intelligence Testing at Government Training Centres', 1941, *Unpublished I.H.R.B. Report*.

3a Yates, A., and Pidgeon, D. A., *Admission to Grammar Schools*, Newnes Educational Publishing, Co. Ltd., 1957.

b Vernon, P. E., *Secondary School Selection*, Methuen, 1957.

4 Massey, T. B., *The Development of Cognitive and Non-cognitive Predictors for the Selection of University Undergraduates*, Ph.D. Dissertation, University of Cambridge (unpublished), 1968.

References

5 Stewart, N., 'AGCT Scores of Army Personnel Grouped by Occupations', *Occupations*, **26**, 1947, 5–41.

6a Terman, L. M., *et. al.*, *Genetic Studies of Genius. I. The Mental and Physical Traits of a Thousand Gifted Children*, Stanford University Press, 1925.

b Terman, L. M., and Oden, M. H., *Genetic Studies of Genius. IV. The Gifted Child Grows Up*, Stanford University Press, 1947.

c Terman, L. M., and Oden, M. H., *Genetic Studies of Genius. V. The Gifted Group at Midlife*, Stanford University Press, 1959.

7 Thorndike, E. L., *The Measurement of Intelligence*, Teachers' College, Columbia University, New York, 1925.

8 Heim, A. W., *The Appraisal of Intelligence*, Methuen, 1954. New edn 1970, N.F.E.R., Chapter 5.

9 Thomson, G., 'General Intelligence: Objectively Determined and Measured', *American Journal of Psychology*, **115**, 1904, 201–92.

10 Vernon, P. E., *Intelligence and Attainment Tests*, University of London Press, 1960.

11 Vernon, P. E., *Personality Assessment*, Methuen, 1964.

12 Butcher, H. J., *Human Intelligence: its Nature and Assessment*, Methuen, 1968.

13 Cronbach, L. J., *Essentials of Psychology Testing*, Harper, New York, 1960.

14 Wiseman, S., *Intelligence and Ability*, Penguin, 1967.

Chapter Thirteen

1a Terman, L. M., *Concept Mastery Test*, Psychological Corporation, 1956.

b Heim, A. W., 'An Attempt to Test High Grade Intelligence', *British Journal of Psychology*, **37**, 1947, 70–81.

c Heim, A. W., *Test AH5*, National Foundation for Educational Research, 1956.

d Heim, A. W., *Test AH 6 AG and SEM*, National Foundation for Educational Research, 1970.

e Raven, J., *Advanced Progressive Matrices*, H. K. Lewis & Co., 1962.

f Valentine, C. W., *Reasoning Test for Higher Levels of Intelligence*, Oliver and Boyd Ltd, 1954.

2 Terman, L. M., and Merrill, M. A., *Stanford-Binet Intelligence Scale*, G. G. Harrap & Co., 1960.

References

3a Wechsler, D., *The Measurement and Appraisal of Adult Intelligence*, Williams and Wilkins, 1958.

b Wechsler, D., *Intelligence Scale for Children*, National Foundation for Educational Research, 1955.

4 Belbin, R. M., *Discovery Learning*, Training Information Pamphlet, Department of Employment and Productivity, 1969.

5 Hardy, G. H., *A Mathematician's Apology*, Cambridge University Press, 1940.

6 Kendall, M. G., 'On the Future of Statistics – a Second Look', *R.S.S. Series A*, **131**, 1968, 182–92.

7a Lehman, H. C., *Age and Achievement*, Oxford University Press, 1953.

b Lehman, H. C., 'More about Age and Achievement', *Gerontologist*, **2**, 1962, 141–8.

c Bromley, D. B., *The Psychology of Human Ageing*, Penguin, 1966, Chapters 12 and 13.

8 De Bono, E., *The Use of Lateral Thinking*, Cape, 1967.

Chapter Fourteen

1 Watts, K. P., 'Influences Affecting the Results of a Test of High Grade Intelligence', *British Journal of Psychology*, **44**, 1953, 359–67.

2 Manton, J., *Elizabeth Garrett Anderson*, Methuen, 1965.

3 Curie, E., *Madame Curie*, Gallimard, Paris, 1938.

4 Levine, J., Fishman, C., and Kagan, J., 'Sex of Child as Determinants of Maternal Behavior', *Paper read at a meeting of the American Ortho-Psychiatric Association*, Washington, D. C., 1967.

5a Mackinnon, D. W., 'The Personality Correlates of Creativity: A Study of American Architects', *International Congress of Applied Psychology. Proceedings*, **XIV**, 1961, 11–39.

b Roe, A., 'Personal Problems in Science', in Taylor, C. W., (ed.), *Third Research Conference on the Identification of Creative Scientific Talent*, University of Utah Press, Utah, 1959.

6a Grygier, T. G., *The Dynamic Personality Inventory*, National Foundation for Educational Research, 1961.

b Stringer, P., 'Masculinity-femininity as a Possible Factor underlying the Personality Responses of Male and Female Art Students', *British Journal of Social and Clinical Psychology*, **6**, 1967, 186–94.

7 Storr, A., *Human Aggression*, Allen Lane The Penguin Press , 1968.

8 Dale, R. R., chapter on Co-education, in Butcher, H. J., (ed.), *Educational Research in Britain*, University of London Press, 1968.

References

9 Andrews, D. M., and Paterson, D. G., *Minnesota Clerical Test Manual*, Psychological Corporation, New York, 1946.

10 Ministry of Transport: *Road Research 1965–66*.

Chapter Fifteen

1 James, W., *Principles of Psychology*, Macmillan, 1901.

2 Watson, J. B., *Psychology from the Standpoint of a Behaviorist*. Lippincott, Philadelphia, 1924.

3a Bartlett, F. C., *Remembering*, Cambridge University Press, 1932.

b Bartlett, F. C., *Thinking*, Allen and Unwin, 1958.

4a Heim, A. W., Watts, K. P., Bower, I. B., and Hawton, K. E., 'Learning and Retention of Word-pairs with Varying Degrees of Association', *Quarterly Journal of Experimental Psychology*, 18, 1966, 193–205.

b Belbin, E., 'The Influence of Interpolated Recall upon Recognition', *Quarterly Journal of Experimental Psychology*, 2, 1950, 163-9.

5a Webb, W. B., 'Some Effects of Prolonged Sleep Deprivation on the Hooded Rat', *Journal of Comparative and Physiological Psychology*, 55, 1962, 791–3.

b Levitt, R. A., and Webb, W. B., 'Effect of Aspartic Acid Salts on Exhaustion Produced by Sleep Deprivation', *Journal of Pharmaceutical Sciences*, 53, 1964, 1125–6.

6 Broadhurst, P. L., *The Science of Animal Behaviour*, Penguin, 1963. This book, among many others, contains descriptions of experiments (c), (d) and (e).

7 Bradford Hill, A., 'An Investigation into the Sickness Experience of London Transport Workers, with Special Reference to Digestive Disturbances', *Medical Research Council Industrial Health Research Board Report No. 79*, H.M. Stationery Office, 1937.

8a Mischel, W., *Personality and Assessment*, Wiley, 1968, Chapters 1–3.

b Vernon, P. E., *Personality Assessment: a Critical Survey*, Methuen, 1964.

Index

Index

Index of Authors

Index of Authors

More about Penguins
and Pelicans

Penguinews, which appears every month, contains
details of all the new books issued by Penguins as they
are published. From time to time it is supplemented by
Penguins in Print, which is a complete list of all books
published by Penguins which are in print. (There are well
over four thousand of these.)

A specimen copy of *Penguinews* will be sent to you free on
request. For a year's issues (including the complete
lists) please send 30p if you live in the United
Kingdom, or 60p if you live elsewhere. Just write to Dept
EP, Penguin Books Ltd, Harmondsworth, Middlesex,
enclosing a cheque or postal order, and your name will be
added to the mailing list.

Note: *Penguinews* and *Penguins in Print* are not available
in the U.S.A. or Canada